ANTI-INFLAMMATORY
COOKBOOK FOR
BEGINNERS

Countless Easy and Delicious Recipes to Detox your Body,
Reduce Inflammation, and Strengthen Immune System.
Boost your Well-being with the 12-Week Meal Plan

D1205641

ANTI INFLAMMATORY COOKBOOK FOR BEGINNERS

ISBN: 979-8391068266

10 9 8 7 6 5 4 3 2 1

GET YOUR BONUS

THE DIGITAL VERSION OF "PLANT BASED COOKBOOK"
BY MELISSA JEFFERSON IS 100% FREE.
YOU DON'T NEED TO ENTER ANY DETAILS EXCEPT
YOUR NAME AND EMAIL ADDRESS.

PLANT BASED

Tasty and Easy Plant-Based
Recipes to Boost Your Well-Being,
Improve your Energy,
and Feel Lighter

To download your bonus scan the QR code below or go to

https://bonus4books.com/melinda-jefferson-ai

SCAN ME

TABLE OF CONTENTS

INTRODUCTION

Anti-Inflammatory Diet Fundamentals

These days, the anti-inflammatory diet is all the rage, but it's not a fad. To begin, an anti-inflammatory diet emphasizes eating whole, natural foods as much as possible to support a healthy inflammatory response in your body. Reduce your chances of chronic bodily pains, persistent indigestion, and illnesses like fibromyalgia, heart disease, and cancer by lowering inflammation in your body.

So, what is inflammation precisely, and why are you trying to prevent it?

You've probably encountered inflammation if you've ever had a cold, injured your ankle, or skinned your knee. Your body's normal and essential reaction to external stresses such as damage or illness. The reaction normally switches off after your body gets the stressor under control. When the inflammatory response does not cease functioning and continues to operate long after the initial need has passed, it may result in harmful chronic inflammation.

You'll be well on your way to encouraging a healthy inflammatory response if you regularly eat foods like vividly colored fruits and vegetables, herbs and spices, and healthy fats.

It would help if you avoided or restricted meals that might create a detrimental inflammatory response and consume anti-inflammatory nutrients.

Refined carbs, such as crackers, cakes, and bagels; foods containing gluten meals with added sugars; and foods containing Tran's fats, such as fried foods, are all known to induce inflammation.

How It Works?

The anti-inflammatory diet is defined as a specific diet to fight latent inflammations in your body entirely naturally.

In fact, the anti-inflammatory diet essentially has species of natural or vegetable origin as ingredients. In reality, it is not a vegan or vegetarian diet as some products of animal origin are allowed, but always in very moderate quantities and especially in distant moments.

In fact, your first goal will be to have a balanced diet, that is, tailored to your habits and your work, family, and personal activities.

You do not have to overdo the food you introduce in each meal. Still, it is good to spread the quantities (and calories) over several meals or at different times.

Excess calories and their consequent non-disposal cause severe problems for your body, primarily overweight and obesity.

Today, these two diseases are one of the leading causes of death in our country, or, in general, they are diseases that lead to other secondary conditions that can cause severe discomfort (such as inflammation) and generate a period of depression.

So, the first step you need to consider is to significantly reduce the calories introduced into your diet and try to have a correct calorie intake, i.e., neither too high nor too low.

Another aspect that needs to be taken care of is eating habits. We are often used to eating out of hours, or when we should have a simple snack, we find ourselves ingesting large portions of a given food. Consequently, our metabolism is compromised.

You will need to determine which eating habits suit your overall health and tailor them to your lifestyle.

With practice and time, you will soon realize that the anti-inflammatory diet is your best ally against inflammation. Hence, the real benefits you will perceive in the concise term. While in the long run, you will notice a strong feeling of positivity and well-being as well as, of course, weight loss and its stabilization. In fact, it is essential not to be fluctuating with weight, that is, not to lose and gain weight in a short time, but it is always better to be constant and have a weight that does not fluctuate too much.

Constant weight will help you reach your health goals first, and then write down what your target weight or ideal weight should be.

Constantly monitoring your weight is essential, and so is its stabilization.

An anti-inflammatory diet is an excellent tool to stabilize your weight and regain your ideal weight. In fact, the anti-inflammatory diet will allow you to feel good immediately and give yourself (why not) some whim.

Chronic Inflammation and Health Risks

Chronic inflammation is type of inflammation is the type of inflammation, which is bad for you. While acute inflammation following an injury or infection is good for you and to be encouraged, sometimes inflammation has nothing to do with any injury or infection. Sometimes an inflammatory response stays for far too long after an infection has been combated making the body to switch on a mode where it is always reacting as if it is under attack. The constant activation of the immune system exhausts the entire body and affects the effectiveness of white blood cells something, which can further result to the malfunctioning of these immune system. This might in turn bring about symptoms such as headaches, skin outbreaks, loss of joint function, congestion, dry eyes, diarrhea, fever, chills, fatigue, loss of energy, swelling, body aches and severe pains etc. You might also develop such complications like cancer, diabetes, arthritis and various other problems.

From the above explanation, it is clear that chronic inflammation is a term, which describes inflammation that can last several months or even years. It may result from:

• An autoimmune response to a self antigen – this is where the immune system attacks healthy tissues after mistaking them for harmful pathogens

• Your inability to deal with acute inflammation (by eliminating the cause) and

• A persistent, low intensity chronic irritant

How Do I Know if I Have Inflammatory Issues?

There are several things that might make your body more prone to inflammatory reactions. These factors include:

• **Diet:** Saturated or trans fats—which are found in dairy, red meat, baked goods, and fried foods—are associated with higher levels of inflammation-causing molecules in the body. The same is true for refined sugar and highly processed foods.

• **Age:** As we get older, we produce more inflammation-causing molecules in our bodies.

• **Stress and sleep disorders:** This is an important one to consider because stress is a big problem for many people around the world. Modern life has become extremely fast paced and can be very demanding on our health. Emotional and physical stress can cause increased production of inflammation-causing molecules. Irregular sleeping patterns can have the same effect.

• **Obesity:** Studies have shown a connection between high levels of fatty tissue and the production of inflammation-causing molecules (Pahwa et al., 2019). Some of these studies have found that fat levels and inflammation-causing molecules increase proportionally.

• **Low levels of sex hormones:** Hormones such as estrogen and testosterone have been found to inhibit the production of inflammation-causing molecules in our bodies. When the levels of these hormones are low, the suppressing effect cannot occur.

• **Smoking:** Smoking cigarettes has been found to decrease the levels of inflammatory-fighting molecules which are needed to keep inflammation levels within a healthy range.

Chronic inflammation can also develop from sensitivity or long-term exposure to an irritant; for example, a chemical in the air.

The common symptoms of chronic inflammation include:

- weight loss or weight gain
- pain in the body
- mood swings, depression, and anxiety
- acid reflux, diarrhea, or constipation
- insomnia and chronic fatigue
- recurrent infections

Diagnosing chronic inflammation can be done with the help of a blood test. Unfortunately, these levels are usually only checked when there is another medical condition present that is causing inflammation. For this reason, many people suffer from chronic inflammation without ever being diagnosed.

What Damage Does Chronic Inflammation Cause?

Most chronic illnesses may be traced back to inflammation, making it a major health concern. Prolonged inflammation can cause the body to mistake its own healthy tissue and organs as harmful and start to attack them, which can lead to a range of autoimmune diseases. According to Pahwa et al. (2019), it is also thought to be linked to other diseases which include:

- **Cancer:** Inflammation plays a role in various types of cancers including ovarian, prostate, pancreatic, kidney, lung, hepatocellular, mesothelioma, and colorectal.

- **Alzheimer's disease:** This presents more in older people as chronic inflammation over time has been shown to decrease cognitive function and can lead to dementia.

- **Cardiovascular disease:** Chronic inflammation can lead to atherosclerosis, which is present when a fatty plaque that is full of cholesterol builds up inside the arteries. Your body can then mistake this plaque for a foreign substance and may respond with inflammation to try to stop the damage. This inflammation can lead to other serious cardiovascular issues such as a stroke.

- **Diabetes:** High levels of body fat can cause chronic inflammation and that changes the way that insulin acts in the body by disrupting insulin-signaling pathways. This can lead to insulin resistance. Chronic inflammation has been said to be at the root of many complications associated with diabetes.

- **Chronic obstructive pulmonary disease (COPD)**: This is a lung disease that presents as a chronic inflammatory response to irritations in the lungs and can lead to long-term issues with breathing.

- **Rheumatoid arthritis:** Those who are genetically predisposed to this condition may develop rheumatoid arthritis due to an autoimmune response to external irritants like smoking. This autoimmune response causes inflammation in the joints which, over time, can cause further complications.

- **Chronic kidney disease**: Inflammation is a common part of this disease. It can lead to inflammation-causing molecules in the blood which further aggravate the disease and can lead to death.

- **Allergic asthma:** This is a chronic inflammatory disorder that can develop if the immune system overresponds and triggers inflammation and tissue remodeling in the airways.

- **Inflammatory bowel disease:** These conditions are characterized by persistent inflammation of the gastrointestinal system.. This can start as ulcerative colitis which causes long-term inflammation as well as ulcers in the rectum or large intestine. Inflammatory bowel disease (IBD) includes Crohn's disease.

Anti-Inflammatory Diet Benefits

People usually do not know much about the anti-inflammatory diet until they themselves experience the symptoms of inflammation. It may even take the development of more serious diseases before people would take the diet more seriously.

While it may be a challenge for beginners, the benefits that come with the diet can help motivate people to know it and implement the diet. Soon enough, those on the anti-inflammatory diet may begin to feel the diet's positive effects. Even people who do not feel body inflammation may apply the anti-inflammatory diet for its preventative qualities.

Weight Loss. Being overweight or obesity is one of the main causes of certain inflammation-related diseases like hepatitis, diabetes, and heart attack, among other diseases. Thus, if one is overweight, the person is at a high risk for acute or chronic inflammation. With the anti-inflammatory diet, one will lose excess weight as the foods that are included in the diet are weight-friendly. It means the foods in the diet do not make one gain weight.

Control of Serious Diseases. It refers to some serious diseases like heart disease and diabetes. If a person has diabetes, the blood sugar is usually fluctuating and this can lead to inflammation. The same holds true for blood cholesterol as high blood cholesterol can cause inflammation and would eventually lead to more serious diseases like heart attacks.

Other serious diseases that may stem from inflammation are certain cancers, asthma, hepatitis, and tuberculosis. With an anti-inflammatory diet, one can control inflammation that causes diseases and the diseases acquired through inflammation.

Control of Aging. With the anti-inflammatory diet, one may also help to control the symptoms of aging. The diet is an excellent anti-aging regimen as inflammation is not only reduced, the toxins that lead to faster aging are also eliminated. The antioxidants found on the anti-inflammatory diet can eliminate toxins. Moreover, applying the diet brings life and glow to one's skin, which is the reason one can successfully control the symptoms of aging.

Psychological and Mental Health. Mental disorders like chronic depression can be adversely affected by inflammation. When one takes in the anti-inflammatory diet, the person can manage and control mental disorders as the diet involves eating antioxidant-rich foods. The antioxidants have a powerful effect on one's psychological and mental health as they eliminate toxins that lead to autoimmune disorders and depression.

Relief of Inflammation Symptoms. Inflammation, when one experiences it, changes the affected area's appearance by swelling and reddening. The annoying part is that inflammation is also painful and such symptoms can affect one's day-to-day activities and they can even take away one's peace of mind.

The thing is that inflammation is internal and, in the organs, like when a person has appendicitis. It cannot be eased externally. Through the diet, one can manage and control the inflammation by eating anti-inflammatory foods so that the symptoms of inflammation can be relieved.

Fights Infection. Infections usually cause inflammation as infections attack the body's cells and tissues. Any kind of infection can attack the body, whether the infection is from an injury or wound or bacterial infection. With the anti-inflammatory diet, the foods to eat have components that can successfully battle infection. When infection is taken care of, the inflammation can also disappear as the cause is eliminated.

Bone and Muscle Diseases Relief. When bones and muscles are inflamed because of diseases like osteoporosis or arthritis, the pain can be annoying. However, with the anti-inflammatory diet, one gradually promotes healing of damaged muscles and relieving pain from bone disease. The foods in the anti-inflammatory diet promote faster healing of the tissues and cells.

Prevention and Healing of 'Silent' Inflammation. 'Silent' inflammation is something that one should watch out for as one will never know if he or she has an inflammation as there are no visible symptoms. The inflammation is internal; thus, there are no swelling and reddening, and one may be shocked later on when the condition worsens. If you want to be sure, maybe you could try the diet. In the event the person may have an internal inflammation, its adverse effects would not continue.

FAQ

Can you consume wine while following an anti-inflammatory diet?

Alcohol is inflammatory when consumed excessively, although red wine in moderation can have antioxidant advantages. "I wouldn't advocate beginning if you don't drink, but red wine has an antioxidant called resveratrol, known to protect against heart disease," Park adds. "There are benefits to red wine when drank in moderation as part of a healthy lifestyle."

How can I combine an anti-inflammatory diet with a healthy lifestyle?

Even 30 minutes of exercise every day has anti-inflammatory properties. The same can be said about getting enough sleep, avoiding smoking, and having time to de-stress and enjoy life.

What are the guidelines for an anti-inflammatory diet?

Choose whole, unprocessed meals like fruits, vegetables, whole grains, legumes (beans, lentils), fish, poultry, nuts, seeds, low-fat dairy, and olive oil to keep inflammation at bay.

How long should you be on an anti-inflammatory diet?

It may take some time for the Anti-Inflammatory diet to be successful. However, try it for at least six weeks, preferably longer. It should eventually become a habit to keep you healthy in the long run. While keeping your glycemic load low, eat more veggies, legumes, whole grains, and fruits.

What does an anti-inflammatory diet consist of?

In a word, it's what you'd expect: a diet high in whole, unadulterated foods. Choose colorful fruits and vegetables such as tomatoes, grapes, berries, cherries, dark green leafy vegetables, fiber-rich whole grains such as oatmeal and brown rice, and legumes such as chickpeas beans, and lentils. Also, look for mono and polyunsaturated fats in healthy fats like olive oil, almonds, and fatty fish.

What meals should you stay away from if you have an inflammatory condition?

Inflammatory foods are highly refined, and they are high in saturated fats. Inflammatory foods include processed meats such as hot dogs and lunch meats and deep-fried vegetables and meats. The same is true for whole milk and whole-milk dairy products; therefore, search for reduced-fat alternatives. Refined carbohydrates and simple sugars, such as white bread, sweets, pastries, soda, sugar, honey, and high fructose corn syrup, are also inflammatory because they promote blood sugar spikes, which cause inflammation.

What is the fastest way to get rid of inflammation in the body?

To reduce inflammation, eat fewer inflammatory meals and more anti-inflammatory foods. Replace processed foods with complete, nutrient-dense meals strong in antioxidants.

Can you cheat on an anti-inflammatory diet?

The present study looked at how rotating between the two diets affected pain and healing from inflammatory damage. According to a new study in mice, people who cheat on their diets on the weekends lose the benefits of healthy eating during the week.

What are the advantages of a low-inflammatory diet?

An anti-inflammatory diet includes items that decrease inflammation while avoiding those that raise it – and for many people trying to minimize internal inflammation, the potential advantages are well worth making the switch. Limiting inflammatory foods decreases your chance of the aforementioned dangerous diseases and can alleviate symptoms of arthritis and irritable bowel syndrome. In addition, weight gain, accelerated aging, mood swings, chronic pain, and cognitive fog. An anti-inflammatory diet is a critical component of this problem.

Anti-Inflammatory Diet Food List

What to Eat

It is vital for a person on the anti-inflammatory diet to know what the recommended foods are in order to keep the person from eating anything else. Moreover, with knowing the right kinds of foods, it would be easy for the person to create his or her specialized meal plan since he or she knows what the right foods are to add to one's meal. Eating the right foods helps in one's health as the person is preventing inflammation's progress and the diseases that inflammation may cause.

Some of the recommended food items are: fruits and vegetables (albeit not all), oils and fats, protein food sources, spices and herbs, seeds and nuts, seafood and fish, whole grains, and beverages.

Oils and Fats. Despite fat getting a bad rap, not all oils are banned from the anti-inflammatory diet, but they should come from healthy sources. Some good sources for fats and oils are herring oil, cod liver oil, sardine oil, salmon oil, sunflower oil, flaxseed oil, olive oil, hazelnut oil, rice bran oil, canola oil, grape seed oil, and walnut oil.

Most of the above-mentioned oils are monounsaturated fatty acids and have omega-3 fatty acids that are heart-friendly. These oils can help reduce one's risk of heart attacks and other inflammation-linked heart diseases. Extra virgin olive oil can fight inflammation and is excellent to alleviate symptoms of asthma and arthritis.

Vegetables and Fruits. These are highly recommended as they are they rich in vitamins, minerals, and antioxidants that promote faster healing; thus, inflammation may be reduced. Recommended fruits are avocados, organic berries, kiwi, grapefruit, cantaloupe, guava, lemons, raw papaya, and cantaloupe. Recommended vegetables are spinach, broccoli, carrots, squash, cabbage, carrots, chard, sweet potato, pumpkin, kale, asparagus, and watercress.

Spices and Herbs. When it comes to reducing inflammation, some spices and herbs are deemed to have positive effects. This is because such spices help to regulate the body's blood sugar levels and relieve pain. Some of the spices and herbs are garlic, turmeric, ginger, onion, cayenne pepper, parsley, paprika, and chili peppers. When eaten raw or used for cooking, the spices can help one to control inflammation.

Protein Food Sources. In the anti-inflammatory diet, red meat should be sparingly consumed. However, protein is an essential component in the diet. Other non-red meat sources are soy beans, tofu, low-fat yogurt, lean chicken meat, eggs, certain seafood, and cheese. Protein is important as it aids cells and tissues during the healing process.

Seafood and Fish. These foods have omega-3 fatty acids and are heart-friendly. They also contain protein that promotes cell regeneration and tissue healing. There is certain seafood that are more potent when it comes to reducing inflammation. They include salmon, mackerel, herring, shad, sardines, roe, oysters, tuna, trout, anchovy, halibut, and even caviar (if one doesn't mind the expense).

Seeds and Nuts. Several varieties of seeds and nuts are said to have protein and omega-3 fatty acids that are good for the heart. The seeds and nuts also have antioxidants to flush toxins away from body. Some of these seeds and nuts are macadamia, flaxseeds, almonds, hazelnuts, cashews, pecans, and Brazil nuts. However, one must make sure that the seeds and nuts have minimal salt as too much sodium can cause inflammation and other health issues.

Beverages. While on the anti-inflammatory diet, one should consume fluids to replenish the body. However, one should not just drink anything. To get rid of inflammation, the best beverages to consume are water (naturally!), low-fat milk, herbal tea, and fresh fruit juices. Water is best as it helps to cleanse the body as well as help the body heal inflamed and damaged tissues and cells. Meanwhile, fresh fruit juices and herbal tea, have antioxidants that help the body rid itself of toxins that can worsen inflammation symptoms.

Whole Grains. Refined grains are a no-no, but unprocessed grains are allowed in the anti-inflammatory diet. Some recommended grains are wheat bran or quinoa.

What to Avoid

The anti-inflammatory diet aims to lessen a person's risk factors in developing inflammation and one of the best ways to do it is to avoid certain foods. In each food group, there are some things that need to be avoided. Thus, there are some vegetables, sugary foods, oils and fats, processed foods, dairy products, refined grains, alcohol, and additives that are 'do-not-eat' items in the anti-inflammatory diet.

Vegetables. There are certain vegetables that contain solanine, which is a known pain trigger for many people. There are vegetables from the nightshade family and some of them are tomatoes and eggplants. While not largely proven, it is all right to limit intake of the nightshade vegetables. If pain is brought on by eating such vegetables, one should not continue to eat them.

Oils and Fats. Unless they come from healthy sources or if they contain omega-6 fatty acids, oils and fats are not recommended. One should stay away from polyunsaturated vegetable oils like corn oil and cottonseed oil. If one has to use oil during cooking, a better alternative is olive oil.

Sugary Foods. Sugar in any forms (refined or raw) is not allowed in the anti-inflammatory diet. This goes for food high in sugar. Why? Sugar is a major cause of diabetes, which leads to inflammation. Sugar also causes tooth decay. In tooth decay, gum inflammation can occur. One should avoid sugar-rich foods like soft drinks, refined juices, candies and pastries. Some healthy sugar substitutes include sweet fruits and honey.

Dairy Products. Many dairy products have allergy triggers that can lead to inflammation, especially to lactose-tolerant individuals. Except for a few dairy items like fat-free dairy products, some of the dairy foods that one should avoid are regular yogurt, cheese, and milk and dairy-containing products like cereals, cakes, butter, sauces, and creams.

Processed Foods. Processed foods like processed meat are unhealthy and they also trigger the symptoms of inflammation. Moreover, many processed foods also have trans-fats that are dangerous to the body. It is be best to avoid luncheon meat, ham, fast food like French fries, junk foods, deep fried foods, and baked goods that are store bought. Instead of eating processed foods, one may be better off eating seafood, chicken, and eggs.

Alcohol. Under no circumstances should one drink alcoholic drinks while he or she is on the anti-inflammatory diet. Alcoholic drinks taste strong and contribute to inflammation especially to the larynx, esophagus, and liver. Thus, alcohol is considered to be a cause for cancer and tumors, particularly liver cancer. One should avoid drinks like wine, gin, whisky, and beer, among other alcoholic drinks. Water is the best substitute for any of them.

Refined Grains. Like processed foods, refined grains have undergone a process that may have changed their natural state. Vitamins and fiber have been considerably reduced. Thus, the grains' anti-inflammatory properties have been greatly reduced and refined grains become inflammation triggers. Refined grain products to avoid are white bread, white flour, noodles, pasta, biscuits, and pastry.

Additives. The most common additive in foods is MSG (monosodium glutamate), which should be avoided while one is on the anti-inflammatory diet. Additives are found in foods like junk foods, store-bought foods, and instant noodles that come with powdered seasonings. Such additives trigger inflammation. Instead of eating foods with restricted additives, one may want to instead use healthier substitutes like herbs, which do not worsen one's health especially if the person is suffering from inflammation.

CHAPTER 1
BREAKFAST

1. Buckwheat Waffles

Preparation time: 15 minutes

Cooking time: 6 minutes

Servings: 2

Ingredients:

- 1/2 cup of brown rice flour
- 1/2 teaspoon of baking soda
- 1 egg
- 1 cup of buckwheat flour
- 1 teaspoon of baking powder
- 1/2 teaspoon of salt
- 1 tablespoon of maple syrup
- 1/2 cup of water
- 1 cup of almond milk
- Coconut oil for the waffle iron
- 1 teaspoon of vanilla extract

Directions:

1. Whisk together the buckwheat flour, baking powder, rice flour, baking soda, and salt in a medium mixing dish.

2. Add the maple syrup, egg, and vanilla to the dry ingredients. Slowly pour in the water and almond milk while continuing to whisk.

3. The batter is absolutely free of lumps.

4. The batter needs 10 minutes to thicken.

5. When the buckwheat is resting, it can settle to the bottom of the dish, so stir thoroughly before using.

6. Garnish the waffle iron with coconut oil and heat it.

7. In the waffle iron, pour the batter and cook according to the manufacturer's instructions.

Per serving: Calories: 282kcal; Protein: 9g; Carbs: 55g; Fat: 4g

2. Anti-inflammatory Porridge

Preparation time: 10 minutes

Cooking time: 25 minutes

Servings: 2

Ingredients:

- ¾ cup Almond Milk, unsweetened
- 2 tbsp. Hemp Seeds
- 2 tbsp. Chia Seeds, whole
- ¼ cup Walnuts, halved
- ¼ cup Almond Butter
- ¼ cup Coconut Flakes, unsweetened & toasted
- ¼ cup Coconut Milk
- ½ tsp. Turmeric Powder
- Dash of Black Pepper, grounded, as needed
- ½ tsp. Cinnamon
- 1 tbsp. Extra Virgin Olive Oil

Directions:

1. To start with, warm a large saucepan across moderate flame.

2. To this, put in the hemp seeds, flaked coconut, and chopped walnuts.

3. Roast for 2 minutes or until toasted.

4. Once the coconut-seed mixture is roasted, transfer to a bowl and set it aside.

5. Then, heat almond milk and coconut milk in a wide saucepan over medium heat.

6. Once it becomes hot but not boiling, remove from the heat. Stir in almond butter and coconut oil to it. Mix.

7. Now, add chia seeds, pepper powder, turmeric powder, and salt to the milk. Combine.

8. Keep it aside for 5 minutes and then add half of the roasted coconut mixture. Mix.

9. Finally, transfer to a serving bowl and top with the remaining coconut mixture.

10. Serve immediately.

11. Tip: If possible, try adding bee pollen for enhanced taste.

Per serving: Calories: 575kcal; Protein: 14.8g; Carbs: 6g; Fat: 50.2g

3. Savory Breakfast Pancakes

Preparation time: 5 minutes

Cooking time: 6 minutes

Servings: 4

Ingredients:

- ½ cup almond flour
- ½ cup tapioca flour
- 1 cup coconut milk
- ½ teaspoon chili powder
- ¼ teaspoon turmeric powder
- ½ red onion, chopped
- 1 handful cilantro leaves, chopped
- ½ inch ginger, grated
- 1 teaspoon salt
- ¼ teaspoon ground black pepper

Directions:

1. First, combine all of the ingredients in a large basin.Heat a pan on low medium heat and grease with oil.

2. Pour ¼ cup of batter onto the pan and spread the mixture to create a pancake.

3. Fry for 3 minutes per side.

4. Repeat until the batter is done.

Per serving: Calories: 108kcal; Protein: 2g; Carbs: 20g; Fat: 2g

4. Mushroom and Bell Pepper Omelet

Preparation time: ten mins

Cooking time: 10 mins

Servings: 2

Ingredients:

- one sliced red bell pepper
- 6 beaten eggs
- one-eighth tsp. ground black pepper
- two tbsps. of additional virgin olive oil
- one cup of sliced mushrooms
- 1/2 a teaspoon of sea salt

Directions:

1. Warmth the olive oil in a broad non-stick pan over medium heat until it shimmers.

2. Combine the mushrooms and red bell pepper in a mixing dish. Cook, stirring regularly, for around 4 minutes, or until tender.

3. Toss simultaneously the salt, eggs, and pepper inside a moderate mixing cup. Establish the eggs over the vegetables and cook for around 3 minutes, or until the edges of the eggs start to prepare.

4. Gently raise the eggs away from the pot's sides with a rubber spatula. Tilting the pan will help the raw egg run to the edges. Cook for 2 to 5 minutes until the edges and core of the eggs are set.

5. Set the omelet in half with a spatula. To eat, break into wedges.

Per serving: Calories: 336kcal; Protein: 18g; Carbs: 7g; Fat: 27g

5. Oats with Berries

Preparation time: 10 minutes

Cooking time: 30 minutes

Servings: 4

Ingredients:

- 1 cup Steel Cut Oats
- Dash of Salt
- 3 cups Water
- For toppings:
- ½ cup Berries of your choice
- ¼ cup Nuts or Seeds of your choice like Almonds or Hemp Seeds

Directions:

1. Place the oats in a small pan and cook them across moderate flame to get started.

2. Now, toast it for 3 minutes while stirring the pan frequently.

3. Next, pour water to the saucepan and mix well.

4. Allow the mixture to boil. Lower the heat.

5. The oats should be cooked and soft in around 23–25 minutes.

6. Once done cooking, transfer the mixture to the serving bowl and top it with the berries and seeds.

7. Serve it warm or cold.

8. Tip: If you desire, you can add sweeteners like maple syrup or or stevia to it.

Per serving: Calories: 118kcal; Protein: 4.1g; Carbs: 16.5g; Fat: 4.4g;

6. Breakfast Burgers with Avocado Buns

Preparation time: ten mins

Cooking time: 5 mins

Servings: 1

Ingredients:

- one ripe avocado
- 1 egg, pasture-raised
- 1 red onion slice
- 1 tomato slice
- 1 lettuce leaf
- Sesame seed for garnish
- Salt, as required

Directions:

1. Then, you need to remove the seed from the avocado. Slice the avocado into half. This will serve as the bun. Set aside.

2. Grease a skillet over medium flame and fry the egg sunny side up for 5 minutes or until set.

3. Assemble the breakfast burger by placing on top of one avocado half with the egg, red onion, tomato, and lettuce leaf. Top with the remaining avocado bun.

4. Garnish with sesame seeds on top and season with salt to taste.

Per serving: Calories: 458kcal; Protein: 13g; Carbs: 20g; Fat: 39g

7. Scrambled Eggs with Smoked Salmon

Preparation time: 10 minutes

Cooking time: 10 minutes

Servings: 2

Ingredients:

- 4 eggs
- 2 tablespoons coconut ilk
- Fresh chives, chopped
- 4 slices of wild-caught smoked salmon, chopped
- salt to taste

Directions:

1. Inside a container, toss the egg, coconut milk, and chives.

2. Grease the skillet with oil and warm across moderate-low flame.

3. Pour the egg mixture and scramble the eggs while cooking.

4. When the eggs start to settle, add in the smoked salmon and cook for 2 more minutes.

Per serving: Calories: 349kcal; Protein: 29g; Carbs: 3g; Fat: 23g

8. Chia Breakfast Pudding

Preparation time: 10 minutes

Cooking time: 25 minutes

Servings: 2

Ingredients:

- 1/2 cup of chia seeds
- 1/2 teaspoon of vanilla extract
- 1/2 cup of chopped cashews, divided
- 1 cup of almond milk
- 1/4 cup of maple syrup or honey
- 1/2 cup of frozen no-added-sugar pitted cherries, thawed, juice reserved, divided

Directions:

1. Combine the chia seeds, almond milk, maple syrup, and vanilla in a quart container with a tight-fitting seal. Set aside after thoroughly shaking.

2. Pour the pudding into two bowls and finish with a quarter cup of cherries and two tablespoons of cashews in each.

Per serving: Calories: 272kcal; Protein: 7g; Carbs: 38g; Fat: 14g

9. Appetizing Crepes with Berries

Preparation time: 15 minutes

Cooking time: 5 minutes

Servings: 4-6

Ingredients:

- 1 cup buckwheat flour
- ½ teaspoon sea salt
- 2 tablespoons coconut oil (1 tablespoon melted)
- 1½ cups almond milk, or water
- 1 egg
- 1 teaspoon vanilla extract
- 3 cups fresh berries, divided
- 6 tablespoons Chia Jam, divided

Directions:

1. Whisk together the buckwheat flour, salt, 1 tablespoon of melted coconut oil, almond milk, egg, and vanilla in a small bowl until smooth.

1. One tablespoon of the coconut oil should be melted and then used to nonstick skillet (12-inch) over medium-high heat. To uniformly distribute the melted oil, tilt the pan.

2. Into the skillet, ladle ¼ cup of batter. To ensure the batter is spread evenly, tilt the pan.

3. Cook for 2 minutes, or until the edges begin to curl up. Toss the crêpe and cook for 1 min on the other end using a spatula.

4. Place the crêpe on a serving dish.

5. Continue to make crêpes with the remaining batter. You should have 5 to 6 crêpes.

6. Spread 1 tablespoon of Chia Jam on 1 crêpe, then top with 1/2 cup of berries.

7. Fold the crêpe over the filling. Repeat with the remaining crêpes and serve.

Per serving: Calories: 242kcal; Protein: 7g; Carbs: 33g; Fat: 11g

10. Healthy Chickpea Scramble Stuffed Sweet Potatoes

Preparation time: 5 minutes

Cooking time: 20 minutes

Servings: 2

Ingredients:

- 1/2 tsp. avocado oil
- 1/2 tsp. turmeric
- 1 cup of chickpeas
- 1/4 small onion (diced)
- 2 cloves of garlic (minced)
- Sea salt
- For the kale:
- half teaspoon avocado oil
- half teaspoon garlic (crushed)
- one cup of kale leaves (stems removed, cut into small pieces)
- For assembling:
- 1/2 avocado (sliced)
- 2 small sweet potatoes (baked)

Directions:

1. In a pan, add the avocado oil over medium heat, along with the garlic and onions.

2. Cook until softened.

3. Add the chickpeas, turmeric, and salt, then continue cooking for about 10 minutes. To avoid drying the mixture out, you may add teaspoons of water.

4. Mash about 2/3 of the chickpeas using a wooden spoon to make a scrambled texture.

5. Set the pan off the heat and set it aside.

6. In a separate pan, add the avocado oil over medium heat, along with the garlic and kale.

7. Cook until soft, then take the pan off the heat.

8. Slice one baked sweet potato in half and use a spoon to scoop out the center.

9. Spoon half of the chickpea scramble into the baked sweet potato and top with half of the softened kale.

10. Top with half of the avocado slices.

11. Repeat the assembling steps for the other baked sweet potato.

12. Serve and enjoy.

Per serving: Calories: 275kcal; Protein: 8.31g; Carbs: 37g; Fat: 11g

11. Cucumber Bites

Preparation time: fifteen mins

Cooking time: 0 mins

Servings: four

Ingredients:

- half cup prepared hummus

- two teaspoons nutritional yeast
- ¼-½ teaspoon ground turmeric
- Pinch of red pepper cayenne
- Pinch of salt
- 1 cucumber, cut diagonally into ¼-½-inch thick slices
- 1 teaspoon black sesame seeds
- Fresh mint leaves, for garnishing

Directions:

1. In a bowl, mix together hummus, turmeric, cayenne and salt.

2. Transfer the hummus mixture in the pastry bag and spread on each cucumber slice.

3. Serve while using garnishing of sesame seeds and mint leaves.

Per serving: Calories: 203kcal; Protein: 8g; Carbs: 20g; Fat: 4g

---

12. Sweet and Savory Breakfast Hash

Preparation time: 10 minutes

Cooking time: 15 minutes

Servings: 2

Ingredients:

- 1/4 tsp. cinnamon
- 1/4 tsp. thyme (dried)
- 1/2 tbsp. coconut oil
- 1/2 lb. ground turkey
- Sea salt
- For the hash:
- 1/4 tsp. garlic powder
- 1/4 tsp. thyme (dried)
- 1/4 tsp. turmeric
- 1/3 tsp. ginger (powdered)
- 1/2 tsp. cinnamon
- half tablespoon coconut oil
- quarter cup of carrots (shredded)
- one cup of butternut squash (cubed, you can also use sweet potato)
- 1 cup of spinach (you can also use other types of greens)
- 1/2 onion (chopped)
- 1 small apple (peeled, cored, chopped)
- 1 small zucchini (chopped)
- Sea salt

Directions:

1. Inside a griddle, warm half of the coconut oil across moderate-high flame.

2. Include the turkey and cook till it's browned.

3. While cooking, season the meat with the spices and mix well.

4. Once cooked, move the turkey onto a plate.

5. Attach the remaining coconut oil into the skillet, along with the onion.

6. Sauté the onion until softened for about 2 to 3 minutes.

7. Add the apple, carrots, squash, and zucchini and cook until softened for about 4 to 5 minutes.

8. Attach the spinach and continue cooking until the leaves wilt.

9. Add the cooked turkey, along with the hash seasonings, and then continue mixing. Taste the hash and adjust the seasonings according to your taste.

10. Place the hash on plates using spoons.

Per serving: Calories: 1284kcal; Protein: 62g; Carbs: 28g; Fat: 103g

13. Coconut Pancakes

Preparation time: ten mins

Cooking time: five mins

Servings: two

Ingredients:

- 1/2 cup of coconut, plus additional as needed
- 1/2 tablespoon of maple syrup
- 1/4 cup coconut flour
- half tsp. salt
- 2 eggs
- half tbsp. coconut oil or almond butter
- 1/2 teaspoon of vanilla extract
- 1/2 teaspoon of baking soda

Directions:

1. Using an electric mixer, combine the coconut milk, maple syrup, eggs, coconut oil, and vanilla in a medium mixing cup.

2. Combine the baking soda, coconut flour, and salt inside a shallow blending container. Establish the dry ingredients with the wet ingredients in a mixing bowl and beat until smooth and lump-free.

3. If the batter is too dense, add more liquid to thin it down to a typical pancake batter consistency.

4. Using coconut oil, lightly grease a big skillet or pan. Preheat the oven to medium-high.

5. Cook until golden brown on the rim. Cook for another 2 minutes.

6. Continue to cook the leftover batter while stacking the pancake on a tray.

Per serving: Calories: 193kcal; Protein: 9g; Carbs: 15g; Fat: 11g

14. Gingerbread Oatmeal

Preparation time: ten mins

Cooking time: 30 mins

Servings: four

Ingredients:

- ¼ tsp. Cardamom, grounded
- 4 cups Water
- ¼ tsp. Allspice
- 1 cup Steel Cut Oats
- 1/8 tsp. Nutmeg
- 1 ½ tbsp. Cinnamon, grounded
- ¼ tsp. Ginger, grounded
- ¼ tsp. Coriander, grounded
- Maple Syrup, if desired
- ¼ tsp. Cloves

Directions:

1. Then, assemble everything in a big pot and cook it over medium, stirring often.

2. Next, cook them for 6 to 7 minutes or until cooked.

3. Once finished, add the maple syrup.

4. Top it with dried fruits of your choice if desired.

5. Serve it hot or cold.

6. Tip: Avoid those spices which you don't prefer.

Per serving: Calories: 175kcal; Protein: 6g; Carbs: 32g; Fat: 32g

15. Smoked Salmon Scrambled Eggs

Preparation time: five mins

Cooking time: 8 mins

Servings: 2

Ingredients:

- 3 ounces flaked smoked salmon
- half teaspoon freshly ground black pepper
- 3/4 tbsp. of extra-virgin olive oil
- 4 beaten eggs

Directions:

1. Heat up the olive oil inside a griddle or pot across moderate-high flame till it starts sparkling.

2. Cook for around 3 minutes, stirring occasionally.

3. Set the eggs and pepper together in a medium mixing cup. Add them to the skillet or pot and cook, stirring gently, for almost five mins, or till cooked.

Per serving: Calories: 236kcal; Protein: 19g; Carbs: 1g; Fat: 18g

16. Granola

Preparation time: 10 minutes

Cooking time: 60 minutes

Servings: 2

Ingredients:

- ½ cup Flax Seeds, grounded
- 1 cup Almonds, whole & raw
- ½ cup Ginger, grated
- 1 cup Pumpkin Seeds, raw
- ½ tsp. Salt
- 1 cup Shredded Coconut, unsweetened
- ¾ cup Water
- 1 cup Oat Bran
- ½ cup Coconut Oil, melted
- 1 cup Dried Cherries, pitted

- 4 tsp. Turmeric Powder

Directions:

1. First, warm up the microwave to 300 degrees Fahrenheit.

2. Next, mix dried cherries, almonds, grounded flax, pumpkin seeds, coconut, salt, and turmeric in a large mixing bowl until mixed well.

3. After that, mix ginger, coconut oil, and water in the blender and blend for 30 to 40 seconds or until well incorporated.

4. Now, spoon in the coconut oil mixture to the nut mixture. Mix well.

5. Pour the mixture onto a baking sheet lined with parchment paper and disperse it across evenly.

6. Bake for 50 to 60 minutes while checking on it once or twice.

7. Enjoy it.

Tip: Substitute dried cherries with raisins if preferred.

Per serving: Calories: 225kcal; Protein: 6g; Carbs: 18g; Fat: 16g

17. Fruity Bowl

Preparation time: 10 minutes

Cooking time: 0 minutes

Servings: 2

Ingredients:

- 2 cups of frozen cherries (pitted)
- 4 dates (pitted and chopped)
- 1 large apple (peeled, cored, and chopped)
- A cup of fresh cherries pitted
- 2 tablespoons of Chia seeds

Directions:

1. Put frozen cherries and dates inside an elevated-speed mixer and beat.

2. Mix the chopped apple with fresh cherries and Chia seeds in a bowl.

3. Add cherry sauce to the puree and stir.

4. Cover and refrigerate them overnight before serving.

Per serving: Calories: 211kcal; Protein: 3.8g; Carbs: 49g; Fat: 3.2g

---

18. Blueberry Breakfast Blend

Preparation time: 8 mins

Cooking time: zero mins

Servings: one

Ingredients:

• one-third tsp turmeric

• 1/2-cup spinach

• 3/4 -cup fresh blueberries

• 1-cup fresh pineapple chunks

• 1-cup water

• 1-Tbsp chia seeds

• 1-Tbsp lemon juice

Directions:

5. Combine all the ingredients in your blender.

6. Blend to a smooth consistency.

Per serving: Calories: 260kcal; Protein: 13g; Carbs: 39g; Fat: 8.6g

---

19. Oatmeal Pancakes

Preparation time: 10 mins

Cooking time: 25 mins

Servings: 2

Ingredients:

• one and a half cups Rolled Oats, whole-grain

• two Eggs, large & pastured

• 2 tsp. Baking Powder

• 1 Banana, ripe

• 2 tbsp. Water

• ¼ cup Maple Syrup

• 1 tsp. Vanilla Extract

• two tbsps. additional Virgin Olive Oil

Directions:

1. To make this delicious breakfast dish, you need to first blend all the ingredients inside an elevated-speed mixer for a minute or two or till you form a uniform batter. Tip: To blend easily, pour egg, banana, and all other liquid ingredients first and finally add oats at the end.

2. Now, take a large skillet and heat it over medium-low heat.

3. Once the skillet is hot, ¼ cup of the batter into it and cook it for three-four mins on each end or till bubbles start appearing in the middle portion.

4. Turn the pancake and cook the other side also.

5. Serve warm.

Per serving: Calories: 201kcal; Protein: 5g; Carbs: 28g; Fat: 8g

---

20. Spinach Fritters

Preparation time: 15 minutes

Cooking time: 5 minutes

Servings: 2-3

Ingredients:

- 2 cups chickpea flour
- ¾ teaspoons white sesame seeds
- ½ teaspoon garam masala powder
- ½ teaspoon red chili powder
- ¼ teaspoon ground cumin
- 2 pinches of baking soda
- Salt, to taste
- 1 cup water
- 12-14 fresh spinach leaves
- Olive oil, for frying

Directions:

1. Inside a large container, include the entire components excluding spinach and oil and combine until an easy mixture forms.

2. Within a sizable griddle, warm oil on moderate flame.

3. Dip each spinach leaf in chickpea flour mixture evenly and place in the hot oil in batches.

4. Cook, flipping occasionally for around three-five mins or until golden brown from each side.

5. Transfer the fritters onto paper towel lined plate.

Per serving: Calories: 211kcal; Protein: 9g; Carbs: 13g; Fat: 2g

CHAPTER 2
SOUPS

21. Zesty Broccoli Soup

Preparation time: ten mins

Cooking time: twenty mins

Servings: four

Ingredients:

- one tbsp. ghee
- one average white onion, chopped
- three garlic cloves, crushed
- one head broccoli, unevenly sliced
- one carrot, sliced
- one celery stalk, chopped
- three cups vegetable broth
- half tsp. salt
- half tsp. freshly embraced lemon juice
- half tsp. lemon zest
- Newly ground black pepper

Directions:

1. Ghee should be melted across a flame setting of moderate inside a large soup saucepan.

2. Fry the onion and garlic for five mins. Place them in the pan.

3. Include the vegetables and cook for two mins, stirring occasionally.

4. Add the broth, salt, lemon juice, lemon zest, as well as pepper and stir to combine.

5. Reduce heat to low and simmer for ten minutes.

6. Serve immediately.

Per serving: Calories: 80kcal; Protein: 2g; Carbs: 10g; Fat: 4g

22. Squash Green Pea Soup

Preparation time: 5 minutes

Cooking time: 50 minutes

Servings: 7

Ingredients:

- 5 cups butternut squash, skinned, seeded, and cubed
- 5 cups low-sodium chicken broth
- Topping:
- 2 cups fresh green peas
- Two tablespoons fresh lime juice
- Black pepper, as required

Directions:

1. Begin by warming the broth and squash in the pot on moderate heat.

2. Let it simmer for approximately 45 minutes, then add the black pepper, lime juice, and green peas.

3. Cook for another 5 minutes, then allow it to cool.

4. Puree the soup using the handheld blender until smooth.

5. Serve.

Per serving: Calories: 152kcal; Protein: 4.2g; Carbs: 31g; Fat: 3.7g

23. Taco Soup

Preparation time: 15 mins

Cooking time: 8 hrs

Servings: six

Ingredients:

- one lb. ground turkey breast
- 1 onion, chopped

- 1 can tomatoes and green chilis, with their juice
- 6 cups Poultry Broth or store-bought
- one tsp. chili powder
- one tsp. ground cumin
- half tsp. of sea salt
- ¼ cup chopped fresh cilantro
- Juice of 1 lime
- ½ cup grated low-Fat: Cheddar cheese

Directions:

1. Crumble the turkey into the slow cooker. Add the onion, tomatoes, green chilis (with their juice), broth, chili powder, cumin, and salt. Cover and cook on low within 8 hrs.

2. Stir in the cilantro and lime juice. Serve garnished with the cheese.

Per serving: Calories: 281kcal; Protein: 30g; Carbs: 20g; Fat: 10g

24. Roasted Red Pepper and Eggplant Soup

Preparation time: twenty mins

Cooking time: forty mins

Servings: six

Ingredients:

- One small sweet onion, sliced into quarters
- Two small red bell peppers shared
- two cups cubed eggplant
- Two garlic cloves, minced
- One tablespoon olive oil
- one cup Easy Chicken Stock
- Water
- quarter cup sliced fresh basil
- Newly ground black pepper

Directions:

1. Warm up the microwave to 350 degrees F.

2. Put the onions, red peppers, eggplant, and garlic in a large ovenproof baking dish.

3. Spread some olive oil over the veggies.

4. Roast the vegetables for around 30 minutes or while waiting until they are mildly overcooked and tender.

5. Cool the vegetables mildly and remove the skin from the peppers.

6. Purée the vegetables in batches inside a mixing bowl (or within a big container, utilizing a handheld immersion mixer) with the chicken stock.

7. Transfer the soup to a medium-sized pan, and then include water little by little until it reaches the required consistency. The basil should be added after the broth has been brought to a boil.

8. Season with pepper and serve.

Per serving: Calories: 61kcal; Protein: 2g; Carbs: 9g; Fat: 2g

25. Beef & Vegetable Soup

Preparation time: 5 mins

Cooking time: 55 mins

Servings: 4

Ingredients:

- one lb. beef stew
- three and a half cups water
- one cup raw sliced onions
- ½ cup of frozen green peas
- One teaspoon black pepper
- ½ cup frozen okra

- ½ teaspoon basil
- ½ cup frozen carrots, diced
- ½ teaspoon thyme
- ½ cup of frozen corn

Directions:

1. Put a big pot across moderate flame, then include the beef, water, thyme, basil, and black pepper.

2. Cook the beef for 45 minutes on a simmer.

3. Stir in the okra and other vegetables and cook until the meat is al dente.

4. Serve warm.

Per serving: Calories: 163kcal; Protein: 8g; Carbs: 19.3g; Fat: 6.5g

26. Chicken Squash Soup

Preparation time: 15 minutes

Cooking time: 5 hours & 30 minutes

Servings: 3

Ingredients:

- ½ Butternut Squash (large)
- 1 clove Garlic
- 1 ¼ quarts broth (vegetable or chicken)
- 1/8 tsp. Pepper (white)
- ½ tbsp. chopped Parsley
- 2 minced Sage leaves
- 1 tbsp. Olive Oil
- ¼ chopped onion (white)
- 1/16 tsp. Black Pepper (cracked)
- 1/2 tbsp. of Pepper Flakes (chili)
- ½ tsp. chopped rosemary

Directions:

1. Warm up the microwave to 400 degrees. Oil a baking tray. Prepare a preheated oven to roast the squash for 30 minutes.

2. Transfer it to a plate and let it cool. Sauté onion and garlic in the oil.

3. Now, scoop out the flesh from the roasted squash and add to the sautéed onion & garlic. Mash all of it well. Pour ½ quart of the broth into the slow cooker. Add the squash mixture. Cook on "low" for 4 hrs. Using a blender, make a smooth puree.

4. Transfer the puree to the slow cooker. Add in the rest of the broth and other ingredients. Cook again for 1 hr. on "high". Serve in heated soup bowls.

Per serving: Calories: 158kcal; Protein: 3g; Carbs: 24g; Fat: 3g

27. Stuffed Pepper Soup

Preparation time: 15 minutes

Cooking time: 8 hours & 10 minutes

Servings: 6

Ingredients:

- 1 lb. ground Beef (drained)
- 1 chopped onion (large)
- 2 cups Tomatoes (diced)
- 2 chopped Green Peppers
- 2 cups Tomato Sauce
- 1 tbs. Beef Bouillon
- 3 cups of water
- Pepper
- 1 teaspoon Salt
- one cup cooked rice (white)

Directions:

1. Place the entire components inside a cooker. Cook for 8 hours on "low." Serve hot.

Per serving: Calories: 216.1kcal; Protein: 18.3g; Carbs: 21.8g; Fat: 5.2g

28. Golden Mushroom Soup

Preparation time: 15 minutes

Cooking time: 8 hours

Servings: 6

Ingredients:

- 1 onion, finely chopped
- 1 carrot, peeled and finely chopped
- 1 fennel bulb, finely chopped
- 1-pound fresh mushrooms, quartered
- 8 cups Vegetable Broth, Poultry Broth, or store-bought
- ¼ cup dry sherry
- 1 teaspoon dried thyme
- 1 tsp. garlic powder
- half tsp. sea salt
- one-eighth tsp. newly ground black pepper

Directions:

1. Put all the ingredients in the slow cooker and stir them together.

2. Cover and set on low. Cook for 8 hours.

Per serving: Calories: 71kcal; Protein: 3g; Carbs: 15g; Fat: 0g

29. Brown Rice and Chicken Soup

Preparation time: 15 mins

Cooking time: four hrs

Servings: four

Ingredients:

- 1/3 cups Brown Rice
- 1 chopped Leek
- 1 sliced Celery Rib
- 1 ½ cups water
- ½ tsp. Kosher Salt
- ½ Bay Leaf
- 1/8 tsp. Thyme (dried)
- ¼ tsp. Black Pepper (ground)
- 1 tbsp. chopped parsley
- ½ quart Chicken Broth (low sodium)
- 1 sliced Carrot
- ¾ lb. of Chicken Thighs (skin and boneless)

Directions:

1. Boil 1 cup of water with ½ tsp. of salt in a saucepan. Add the rice. Cook for 30 mins on medium flame. Brown chicken pieces in the oil. Transfer the chicken to a plate when done.

2. In the same pan, sauté the vegetables for 3 mins. Now, place the chicken pieces in the slow cooker. Add water and broth. Cook on "low" for 3 hrs. Put the rest of the fixing, the rice last. Cook again for 10 mins on "high." After discarding Bay leaf, serve in soup bowls

Per serving: Calories: 208kcal; Protein: 2g; Carbs: 18g; Fat: 1g

30. Coconut Cashew Soup with Butternut Squash

Preparation time: ten mins

Cooking time: twenty mins

Servings: six

Ingredients:

- two tbsps. coconut oil
- three-quarter cup grilled cashews
- two red chili peppers, sowed & chopped

- three garlic cloves, skinned & crushed
- one white onion, chopped
- one and a half tbsps. Ginger, skinned & crushed
- two carrots, sliced
- one small butternut squash, shared, chopped
- one small Napa cabbage, ragged
- two cups green beans, clipped
- three cups vegetable broth
- one (fourteen oz.) tin full-Fat: coconut milk
- half teaspoon salt
- Newly ground black pepper
- one cup mung bean sprouts
- four tbsps. grilled coconut shavings

Directions:

1. Coconut oil should be melted over a flame setting of moderate inside a large soup saucepan.

2. Place the walnuts in a pan and cook them for two mins. Pull it out of the skillet and put it to the end.

3. Place the peppers, garlic, and onion into the pan, and fry for a minimum of six mins. After that, add the ginger and carrots, and sauté them for around three mins, or till the carrots and zucchini start to become more pliable.

4. Mix together the ragged cabbage, green beans, stock, coconut milk, salt, and pepper, and then mix with the other ingredients. Boil for fifteen mins. Remove the pot from the fire.

5. Bean sprouts and coconut shavings should be stirred in at this point.

6. After pouring into containers, the broth should be served instantly.

Per serving: Calories: 340kcal; Protein: 7g; Carbs: 23g; Fat: 25g

31. Roasted Carrot Soup

Preparation time: 15 minutes

Cooking time: 50 minutes

Servings: 4

Ingredients:

- 8 large carrots, washed and peeled
- 6 tablespoons olive oil
- 1-quart broth
- Cayenne pepper to taste
- Sunflower seeds and pepper to taste

Directions:

1. Warm your oven to 425 degrees F. Take a baking sheet, add carrots, drizzle olive oil, and roast for 30-45 minutes. Put roasted carrots into a blender and add broth, puree. Pour into saucepan and heat soup. Season with sunflower seeds, pepper and cayenne. Drizzle olive oil. Serve and enjoy!

Per serving: Calories: 222kcal; Protein: 5g; Carbs: 7g; Fat: 18g

32. Italian Wedding Soup

Preparation time: 15 minutes

Cooking time: 7 hours

Servings: 6

Ingredients:

- 1-pound ground turkey breast
- 1½ cups cooked Brown Rice
- 1 onion, grated

- ¼ cup chopped fresh parsley
- 1 egg, beaten
- one tsp. garlic powder
- one tsp. sea salt, divided
- 6 cups Poultry Broth or store-bought
- one-eighth tsp. newly ground black pepper
- Pinch red pepper flakes
- 1-pound kale, tough stems removed, leaves chopped

Directions:

1. Inside a small container, mix the turkey breast, rice, onion, parsley, egg, garlic powder, and ½ teaspoon of sea salt. Roll the mixture into ½-inch meatballs and put them in the slow cooker.

2. Add the broth, black pepper, red pepper flakes, and the remaining ½ teaspoon of sea salt. Conceal then cook on low for seven to eight hrs. Prior to offering, mix in the kale. Cover and cook till the kale wilts.

Per serving: Calories: 302kcal; Protein: 29g; Carbs: 29g; Fat: 7g

33. Chicken Noodle Soup

Preparation time: 5 mins

Cooking time: 45 mins

Servings: six

Ingredients:

- one lb. chicken, sliced into parts
- One teaspoon red pepper
- ¼ cup lemon juice
- One teaspoon caraway seed

- 3 ½ cups water
- One teaspoon oregano
- One tablespoon poultry seasoning
- 1/8 teaspoon stevia
- One teaspoon garlic powder
- ½ cup celery
- One teaspoon onion powder
- ½ cup green pepper
- Two tablespoons vegetable oil
- 1 cup egg noodles
- One teaspoon black pepper

Directions:

1. First, rub the chicken with lemon juice and place it in a large pot.

2. Add water, vegetable oil, all the spices, herbs, and the red pepper.

3. Cover the chicken soup and cook for about 30 minutes.

4. Stir in the noodles along with the other ingredients and cook for 15 minutes.

5. Serve.

Per serving: Calories: 213kcal; Protein: 23.9g; Carbs: 10g; Fat: 7.7g

34. Chipotle Squash Soup

Preparation time: 15 minutes

Cooking time: 4 hours & 20 minutes

Servings: 6

Ingredients:

- 6 cups Butternut Squash (cubed)
- ½ cup chopped Onion
- 2 tsp. Adobo Chipotle
- two cups Chicken Broth

- one tablespoon Brown Sugar
- ¼ cup Tart Apple (chopped)
- one cup Yogurt (Greek style)
- 2 tbsp. Chives (chopped)

Directions:

1. Except for yogurt, chives, and apple, place the entire components in the slow cooker. Cook on "low" for four hrs. Now, in a blender or food processer, puree the cooked ingredients. Transfer puree to slow cooker.

2. Put the yogurt and cook on "Low" within 20 more mins. Garnish with chives and apples. Serve hot in heated bowls.

Per serving: Calories: 102kcal; Protein: 2g; Carbs: 22g; Fat: 1g

35. Chicken and Tortilla Soup

Preparation time: 15 mins

Cooking time: 6 hrs

Servings: 12

Ingredients:

- 3 Chicken Breasts (boneless and skinless)
- 15 ounces diced Tomatoes
- 10 ounces Enchilada Sauce
- 1 chopped onion (med.)
- 4 ounces chopped Chili Pepper (green)
- 3 minced cloves Garlic
- 2 cups Water
- 14.5-ounces Chicken Broth (fat-free)
- 1 tbsp. Cumin
- 1 tbs. Chile Powder
- 1 tsp. Salt
- ¼ tsp. Black Pepper
- Bay Leaf
- 1 tbsp. Cilantro (chopped)
- 10 ounces Frozen Corn
- 3 tortillas, cut into thin slices

Directions:

1. Put all the listed fixing in the slow cooker. Stir well to mix.

2. Cook on low heat within 8 hrs. or high heat for 6 hrs. Shred the chicken breasts to a plate.

3. Add chicken to other ingredients.

4. Serve hot, garnished with tortilla slices.

Per serving: Calories: 93.4kcal; Protein: 8.1g; Carbs: 11.5g; Fat: 1.6g

CHAPTER 3
BEANS AND GRAINS

36. Celery and Turmeric Lentils

Preparation time: 10 minutes

Cooking time: 10 minutes

Servings: 4

Ingredients:

- 2 tablespoons olive oil
- 1 celery stalk, chopped
- one onion, sliced
- one tablespoon ground turmeric
- one teaspoon garlic powder
- one (fourteen-ounce / 397-g) tin lentils, wearied
- one (fourteen-ounce / 397-g) tin diced tomatoes
- Sea salt and pepper, as required

Directions:

1. Warm the olive oil inside a pan over medium heat and place the onion, celery, and turmeric.

2. Cook for five mins until tender. Mix in garlic powder, lentils, tomatoes, salt, and pepper and cook for five more mins.

3. Offer immediately.

Per serving: Calories: 285kcal; Protein: 16g; Carbs: 35g; Fat: 9g

37. Grandma's Black Bean Chili

Preparation time: 15 mins

Cooking time: twenty mins

Servings: 4

Ingredients:

- two tbsps. olive oil
- one teaspoon smoked paprika
- 1 onion, chopped
- 2 (28-ounce / 794-g) cans diced tomatoes
- 2 (14-ounce / 397-g) cans black beans
- 1 chili pepper, chopped
- 1 teaspoon garlic powder
- ½ teaspoon sea salt

Directions:

1. Warm the olive oil inside a pot across moderate flame, place the onion, and cook for five mins till tender.

2. Mix in tomatoes, black beans, chili pepper, garlic powder, smoked paprika, and salt and raise to a boil. Then low the flame and cook for 15 more mins. Serve warm.

Per serving: Calories: 338kcal; Protein: 17g; Carbs: 54g; Fat: 9g

38. Garbanzo And Kidney Bean Salad

Preparation time: 10 minutes

Cooking time: 0 minutes

Servings: 4

Ingredients:

- 1 (15 ounce) can kidney beans, drained
- 1 (15.5 ounce) can garbanzo beans, drained
- 1 lemon, zested and juiced
- 1 medium tomato, chopped
- 1 teaspoon capers, rinsed and drained
- 1/2 cup chopped fresh parsley
- 1/2 teaspoon salt, or to taste
- 1/4 cup chopped red onion
- 3 tablespoons extra virgin olive oil

Directions:

1. Inside a salad container, toss well lemon juice, olive oil and salt until dissolved.

2. Stir in garbanzo, kidney beans, tomato, red onion, parsley, and capers. Toss well to coat.

3. Allow flavors to mix for 30 minutes by setting in the fridge.

4. Mix again before serving.

Per serving: Calories: 329kcal; Protein: 12.1g; Carbs: 46.6g; Fat: 12.0g

39. Rice & Currant Salad Mediterranean Style

Preparation time: 20 minutes

Cooking time: 50 minutes

Servings: 4

Ingredients:

- 1 cup basmati rice
- salt
- 2 1/2 Tablespoons lemon juice
- 1 teaspoon grated orange zest
- 2 Tablespoons fresh orange juice
- 1/4 cup olive oil
- 1/2 teaspoon cinnamon
- Salt and pepper to taste
- 4 chopped green onions
- 1/2 cup dried currants
- 3/4 cup shelled pistachios or almonds
- 1/4 cup chopped fresh parsley

Directions:

1. Place a nonstick pot on medium high fire and add rice. Toast rice until opaque and starts to smell, around 10 minutes.

2. Add 4 quarts of boiling water to pot and 2 tsp salt. Boil until tender, around 8 minutes uncovered.

3. The rice should be drained and allowed to cool fully in a single layer on a baking sheet.

4. In a large salad bowl, whisk well the oil, juices and spices. Add salt and pepper to taste.

5. Add half of the green onions, half of parsley, currants, and nuts.

6. Mix with the rice when it has cooled, and then let it aside for at least 20 minutes.

7. If needed adjust seasoning with pepper and salt.

8. Garnish with remaining parsley and green onions.

Per serving: Calories: 450kcal; Protein: 9.0g; Carbs: 50.0g; Fat: 24.0g

40. Basic Beans

Preparation time: 30 mins

Cooking time: seven-eight hrs

Servings: 6 cups

Ingredients:

- one lb. dried beans, soaked for at least 8 hours
- Water

Directions:

1. Drain and rinse the beans well. Put them in slow cooker and cover with 2 inches of fresh water.

2. Cover then cook on low for 7 to 8 hours, or until soft and cooked through. Drain and serve.

Per serving: Calories: 259kcal; Protein: 15g; Carbs: 48g; Fat: 0g

41. Herbed Harvest Rice

Preparation time: 15 minutes

Cooking time: 3 hours

Servings: 4 to 6

Ingredients:

• 2 cups brown rice, soaked in water overnight, drained, and rinsed

• ½ small onion, chopped

• 4 cups vegetable broth

• two tbsps. additional-virgin olive oil

• half tsp. dried thyme leaves

• ½ tsp. garlic powder

• ½ cup cooked sliced mushrooms

• ½ cup dried cranberries

• ½ cup toasted pecans

Directions:

1. Inside slow cooker, mix the rice, onion, broth, olive oil, thyme, and garlic powder. Toss well.

2. Conceal then cook on high for 3 hours.

3. Include the mushrooms, cranberries, and pecans, and mix to combine.

Per serving: Calories: 546kcal; Protein: 10g; Carbs: 88g; Fat: 20g

---

42. Spanish Rice

Preparation time: 15 minutes

Cooking time: 5 to 6 hours

Servings: 4 to 6

Ingredients:

• 2 cups white rice

• 2 cups vegetable broth

• 2 tbsps. additional-virgin olive oil

• 1 (14½-ounce / 411-g) can crushed tomatoes

• one (four oz. / 113-g) tin Hatch green chiles

• half average onion, chopped

• 1 teaspoon sea salt

• ½ tsp. ground cumin

• half tsp. garlic powder

• half tsp. chili powder

• ½ tsp. dried oregano

• Newly ground black pepper, to taste

Directions:

1. Inside slow cooker, combine the entire components and mix.

2. Cover then cook on low for 5 to 6 hours, fluff, and serve.

Per serving: Calories: 406kcal; Protein: 8g; Carbs: 79g; Fat: 7g

---

43. Mushroom Risotto with Spring Peas

Preparation time: fifteen mins

Cooking time: 2-3 hrs

Servings: four to six

Ingredients:

• 1½ cups Arborio rice

• one cup English peas

• one small shallot, minced

• ¼ cup dried porcini mushrooms

• 4½ cups broth of choice (choose vegetable to keep it vegan)

• 1 tablespoon freshly squeezed lemon juice

• ½ tsp. garlic powder

• half tsp. sea salt

Directions:

1. Inside slow cooker, mix all the ingredients and stir to mix well.

2. Cover then cook on high for 2 to 3 hours and serve.

Per serving: Calories: 382kcal; Protein: 12g; Carbs: 79g; Fat: 1g

44. Hot Coconut Beans with Vegetables

Preparation time: 15 mins

Cooking time: ten mins

Servings: four

Ingredients:

- two tablespoons olive oil
- one onion, chopped
- 1 red bell pepper, chopped
- 2 garlic cloves, minced
- 1 tablespoon hot powder
- 1 (thirteen and a half oz. / 383 gram) tin coconut milk
- two (15½-ounce / 439-g) cans white beans
- one (fourteen and a half oz. / 411 gram) tin chopped tomatoes
- 3 cups fresh baby spinach
- Sea salt and pepper to taste
- Chopped toasted walnuts

Directions:

1. Heat the oil in a pot over medium heat. Place in onion, garlic, hot powder, and bell pepper and fry for five mins, mixing occasionally.

2. Put in the coconut milk and whisk until well mixed.

3. Add in white beans, tomatoes, spinach, salt, and pepper and cook for five mins till the spinach wilts.

4. Garnish with walnuts and serve.

Per serving: Calories: 578kcal; Protein: 11g; Carbs: 48g; Fat: 38g

45. Southern Bean Bowl

Preparation time: 15 minutes

Cooking time: 0 minutes

Servings: 4

Ingredients:

- 1 tomato, chopped
- 1 red bell pepper, chopped
- 1 green bell pepper, chopped
- 1 small red onion, sliced
- 1 (fourteen and a half oz. / 411 gram) tin black-eyed peas
- one (14½-oz. / 411-gram) can black beans
- ¼ cup capers
- 2 avocados, pitted
- 1 tablespoon lemon juice
- ¼ cup sake
- 1 teaspoon dried oregano
- Sea salt to taste
- 2 tablespoons olive oil
- 1 cup leafy greens, chopped

Directions:

1. In a bowl, mix the tomato, peppers, onion, black-eyed peas, beans, and capers.

2. Put the avocados, lemon juice, sake, olive oil, oregano, and salt inside a mixing bowl and blitz till uniform. Include the dressing to the bean container and toss to combine.

3. Top with leafy greens to serve.

Per serving: Calories: 412kcal; Protein: 7g; Carbs: 48g; Fat: 21g

46. White Bean, Chicken & Apple Cider Chili

Preparation time: 20 mins

Cooking time: seven-eight hrs

Servings: four

Ingredients:

- two (fifteen-oz.) white navy beans, drained and washed from cans
- one average onion, sliced
- one (fifteen-oz.) tin chopped tomatoes
- three cups chopped cooked chicken
- 3 cups Chicken Bone Broth or store-bought chicken broth
- one cup apple cider
- two bay leaves
- one tbsp. additional-virgin olive oil
- two tsps. garlic powder
- one tsp. chili powder
- one tsp. sea salt
- half tsp. ground cumin
- quarter tsp. ground cinnamon
- tweak cayenne pepper
- newly ground black pepper
- quarter cup apple cider vinegar

Directions:

1. Put the chicken, beans, onion, tomatoes, broth, cider, bay leaves, chilli powder, garlic powder, cinnamon, cayenne pepper, and black pepper into your slow cooker and stir everything together thoroughly.

2. Turn the heat down low and cover the pot.

3. Cook for seven-eight hrs.

4. Eliminate and remove the bay leaves. Include the apple cider vinegar and stir till combined.

Per serving: Calories: 469kcal; Protein: 51g; Carbs: 46g; Fat: 8g

47. Bean and Rice Casserole

Preparation time: 10 minutes

Cooking time: 35 minutes

Servings: 4

Ingredients:

- 1 cup soaked black beans
- 2 cups water
- 2 teaspoons onion powder
- 2 teaspoons chili powder, optional
- 2 cups brown rice
- 6 ounces (17g;) tomato paste
- 1 teaspoon minced garlic
- 1 teaspoon sea salt

Directions:

1. Combine the entire components in your Instant Pan. Select the "Manual" setting and seal the lid. Cook for 35 mins on increased pressure.

2. When the cooking is finished, let the pressure release for 5 minutes. The next step is to quickly relieve the pressure. In a hot dish.

Per serving: Calories: 444kcal; Protein: 20g; Carbs: 82g; Fat: 4g

48. Brown Rice Pilaf

Preparation time: 5 mins

Cooking time: 10 mins

Servings: four

Ingredients:

- 1 cup low-sodium vegetable broth
- ½ tablespoon olive oil
- one clove garlic, crushed
- one scallion, finely cut
- 1 tablespoon minced onion flakes
- 1 cup instant brown rice
- 1/8 teaspoon newly ground black pepper

Directions:

1. Mix the vegetable broth, olive oil, garlic, scallion, and minced onion flakes in a saucepan and boil. Put rice, then boil it again, adjust the heat and simmer within 10 minutes.

2. Remove and let stand within 5 minutes. Fluff with a fork and season with black pepper.

Per serving: Calories: 100kcal; Protein: 2g; Carbs: 19g; Fat: 2g

49. Habanero Pinto Bean and Bell Pepper Pot

Preparation time: ten mins

Cooking time: 15 mins

Servings: six

Ingredients:

- one teaspoon olive oil
- 2 red bell peppers, diced
- 1 habanero pepper, minced
- 2 (14½-ounce / 411-g) cans pinto beans
- ½ cup vegetable broth
- 1 teaspoon ground cumin
- 1 teaspoon chili powder
- Sea salt and pepper to taste

Directions:

1. Heat the oil in a pot over medium heat.

2. Place in bell and habanero peppers. Sauté for 5 minutes until tender. Add beans, broth, cumin, chili powder, pepper and salt.

3. Raise to a boil afterwards lower the flame then low boil for 10 mins.

Per serving: Calories: 141kcal; Protein: 7g; Carbs: 23g; Fat: 2g

50. Quinoa Salmon Bowl

Preparation time: 15 minutes

Cooking time: 0 minutes

Servings: 4

Ingredients:

- 4 cups cooked quinoa
- 1 pound (45g;) cooked salmon, flaked
- 3 cups arugula
- 6 radishes, thinly sliced
- 1 zucchini, sliced into half moons
- 3 scallions, minced
- ½ cup almond oil
- one tbsp. apple cider vinegar
- one tsp. Sriracha or other hot sauce (or more if you like it spicy)
- 1 teaspoon salt
- ½ cup toasted slivered almonds (optional)

Directions:

1. Combine the quinoa, salmon, arugula, radishes, zucchini, and scallions in a large bowl.

2. Add the almond oil, vinegar, Sriracha, and salt and mix well.

3. Divide the mixture among four serving bowls, garnish with the toasted almonds (if using), and serve.

Per serving: Calories: 790kcal; Protein: 37g; Carbs: 45g; Fat: 52g

51. Coconut Rice with Berries

Preparation time: 10 minutes

Cooking time: 30 minutes

Servings: 2

Ingredients:

- 3/4 cup of water
- 3/4 teaspoon of salt
- 1/2 cup of fresh raspberries or blueberries, divided
- 1/2 cup of shaved coconut, divided
- 1/2 cup of brown basmati rice
- 1/2 cup of coconut milk
- 2 pitted and chopped dates
- 1/4 cup of toasted slivered almonds, divided

Directions:

1. Combine the water, basmati rice, coconut milk, spice, and date pieces inside a moderate pot across increased flame.

2. Stir constantly till the mixture boils. Set the heat to low and cook, occasionally stirring, for 20 to 30 minutes, or until the rice is tender.

3. Place some blueberries, almonds, and coconut on top of each serving of rice.

Per serving: Calories: 281kcal; Protein: 6g; Carbs: 49g; Fat: 8g

52. Spicy Quinoa

Preparation time: 10 minutes

Cooking time: 20 minutes

Servings: 2

Ingredients:

- 1 cup of water
- 1/4 cup of hemp seeds
- 1/2 teaspoon of ground cinnamon
- Pinch salt
- quarter cup of sliced hazelnuts
- half cup of quinoa rinsed well
- 1/4 cup of shredded coconut
- 1 tablespoon of flaxseed
- 1/2 teaspoon of vanilla extract
- 1/2 cup of fresh berries of your choice, divided

Directions:

1. Combine the quinoa & water in a medium saucepan over high heat.

2. Set to a boil, afterwards lower to low heat and continue to cook for 15 to 20 mins until the quinoa is tender.

3. Combine the coconut, flaxseed, hemp seeds, cinnamon, vanilla, and salt in a large mixing bowl.

4. Divide the quinoa into two bowls and finish with some berries and hazelnuts for each serving.

Per serving: Calories: 286kcal; Protein: 10g; Carbs: 32g; Fat: 13g

53. Quick Quinoa with Cinnamon and Chia

Preparation time: 15 minutes

Cooking time: 3 minutes

Servings: 3

Ingredients:

- 2-cups quinoa, pre-cooked
- 1-cup cashew milk
- 1/2-tsp ground cinnamon

- 1-cup fresh blueberries
- 1/4 -cup walnuts, toasted
- 2-tsps raw honey
- 1-Tbsp chia seeds

Directions:

1. Inside a saucepan, add the quinoa and cashew milk. Stir in the cinnamon, blueberries, and walnuts. Cook slowly for three minutes.

2. Take the pan off the stove.

3. Stir in the honey. Garnish with chia seeds on top before serving.

Per serving: Calories: 887kcal; Protein: 29.5g; Carbs: 129g; Fat: 29g

54. Lemon and Cilantro Rice

Preparation time: fifteen mins

Cooking time: 6 hours

Servings: four

Ingredients:

- 3 cups Vegetable Broth (low sodium)
- 1 ½ cups Brown Rice (uncooked)
- Juice of 2 lemons
- 2 tbsp. chopped cilantro

Directions:

1. In a slow cooker, place broth and rice.

2. Cook on "low" for 5 hrs. Check the rice for doneness using a fork.

3. Include the lemon juice and cilantro before serving.

Per serving: Calories: 56kcal; Protein: 1g; Carbs: 12g; Fats 0.3g

55. Healthy Vegetable Fried Rice

Preparation time: 15 minutes

Cooking time: 10 minutes

Servings: 4

Ingredients:

For the sauce:

- 1/3 cup garlic vinegar
- 1½ tablespoons dark molasses
- 1 teaspoon onion powder

For the fried rice:

- 1 teaspoon olive oil
- 2 lightly beaten whole eggs + 4 egg whites
- 1 cup of frozen mixed vegetables
- 1 cup frozen edamame
- 2 cups cooked brown rice

Directions:

1. Make the sauce by mixing the garlic vinegar, molasses, and onion powder inside a glass jar. Shake well.

2. Heat-up oil in a large wok or skillet over medium-high heat. Add eggs and egg whites, let cook until the eggs set, for about 1 minute.

3. Separate the eggs using a spoon or spatula.

4. Add frozen mixed vegetables and frozen edamame. Cook for four mins, mixing regularly.

5. Include the brown rice and sauce to the vegetable-and-egg mixture. Cook for 5 minutes or 'til heated through. Serve immediately.

Per serving: Calories: 210kcal; Protein: 13g; Carbs: 28g; Fat: 6g

CHAPTER 4
MEAT

56. Spiced Ground Beef

Preparation time: ten mins

Cooking time: twenty-two mins

Servings: five

Ingredients:

- two tbsps. coconut oil
- two complete cloves
- two complete cardamoms
- one (two-inch) part cinnamon stick
- two bay leaves
- one tsp. cumin seeds
- two onions, sliced
- Salt, as required
- half tbsp. garlic paste
- half tbsp. new ginger paste
- one lb. lean ground beef
- one and a half tsps. fennel seeds powder
- one tsp. ground cumin
- one and a half tsps. red chili powder
- one-eighth tsp. ground turmeric
- Newly ground black pepper, as required
- one cup coconut milk
- quarter cup water
- quarter cup fresh cilantro, sliced

Directions:

1. Oil should be heated over moderate flame inside a large pot.

2. After adding the cloves, cardamoms, cinnamon stick, bay leaves, and cumin seeds, fry the mixture for approximately twenty to a couple of secs.

3. Fry the onion with two tweaks of salt for around three to four mins after adding it.

4. Fry the garlic-ginger paste for roughly two mins after adding it to the pan.

5. After adding the beef, simmer it for around four to five mins while breaking it up with a spatula.

6. Cook for roughly five mins with the lid on.

7. Cook for roughly two and a half mins and a half while whisking in the spices.

8. Cook for approximately seven to eight mins after stirring in the coconut milk and the water.

9. Add some salt to taste, then remove from the fire.

10. Cilantro should be used as a garnish and the dish should be served warm.

Per serving: Calories: 444kcal; Protein: 39g; Carbs: 29g; Fat: 15g

57. Parsley Pork and Artichokes

Preparation time: ten mins

Cooking time: thirty-five mins

Servings: four

Ingredients:

- two tbsps. balsamic vinegar
- one cup tinned artichoke hearts, wearied
- two tbsps. olive oil
- two lbs. pork stew meat, chopped
- two tbsps. parsley, sliced
- one teaspoon cumin, ground
- one teaspoon turmeric powder
- two garlic cloves, crushed
- tweak of sea salt
- tweak of black pepper

Directions:

1. Inside a skillet heated over moderate flame using the oil, brown the meat for five mins after adding it.

2. To prepare the dish, include the artichokes, vinegar, and the remaining components, then stir the mixture. Cook the mixture for thirty mins across moderate flame, then split it among plates and offer.

Per serving: Calories: 260kcal; Protein: 20g; Carbs: 11g; Fat: 5g

58. Roasted Chicken

Preparation time: sixty mins

Cooking time: sixty mins

Servings: eight

Ingredients:

- half teaspoon thyme
- three pounds complete chicken
- one bay leaf
- three garlic cloves
- four tablespoons Coarsely sliced orange skin
- half teaspoon Black pepper
- half tablespoon salt

Directions:

1. After almost an hr of having it at ambient temp., remove the chicken from the refrigerator.

2. Utilizing paper towels, thoroughly dry the interior as well as the exterior of the chicken.

3. Shorty, when you begin making the chicken seasoning, turn the microwave temperature up to 4500 degrees Fahrenheit.

4. In a low-sided dish, mix the thyme, salt, and pepper together.

5. Apply one third of the seasoning to a swipe and wipe the interior. Place the garlic, citrus peel, and bay leaf inside the chicken before cooking.

6. Fold the wingtips in and knot the legs simultaneously to complete the model. After applying the remaining spice to the chicken, place it onto a roasting pot. Roast the chicken.

7. Place in the microwave and bake for one hour at a temperature of 1600 degrees Fahrenheit.

8. Placed to stay idle for a period of fifteen mins.

9. After the chicken has been roasted, slice it up and serve it.

10. Relish!

Per serving: Calories: 201kcal; Protein: 35.4g; Carbs: 0.8g; Fat: 5.3g

59. Orange Chicken Legs

Preparation time: fifteen mins

Cooking time: eight hrs

Servings: four

Ingredients:

- one orange juice
- quarter cup red vinegar
- A tweak of salt and black pepper
- Zest of one orange
- four chicken legs
- five garlic cloves, crushed
- one red onion, cut finely
- seven oz. tinned peaches, shared
- half cup sliced parsley

Directions:

1. Combine the orange zest with the orange juice, vinegar, salt, and pepper inside a slow cooker. Add the garlic, onion, peaches, and parsley to the slow cooker as well. After adding the chicken, give everything a good stir, then conceal and cook on Low for eight hrs. Split among dishes and offer.

2. Relish!

Per serving: Calories: 251kcal; Protein: 8g; Carbs: 14g; Fat: 4g

60. Pork with Thyme Sweet Potatoes

Preparation time: ten mins

Cooking time: thirty-five mins

Servings: four

Ingredients:

• two sweet potatoes, sliced thinly

• four pork chops

• three spring onions, sliced

• one tbsp. thyme, sliced

• two tbsps. olive oil

• four garlic cloves, crushed

• tweak of sea salt

• tweak of black pepper

• half cup vegetable stock

• half tbsp. chives, sliced

Directions:

1. Mix all the ingredients for the pork chops and potatoes in a roasting pan and mix lightly before roasting for 35 mins at 390°F.

2. Split everything among plates and serve.

Per serving: Calories: 210kcal; Protein: 10g; Carbs: 12g; Fat: 12.2g

61. Pork with Olives

Preparation time: ten mins

Cooking time: forty mins

Servings: four

Ingredients:

• one yellow onion, sliced

• four pork chops

• two tbsps. olive oil

• one tbsp. sweet paprika

• two tbsps. balsamic vinegar

• quarter cup kalamata olives, eroded & sliced

• one tbsp. cilantro, sliced

• tweak of Sea Salt

• tweak of black pepper

Directions:

1. After heating the oil in a skillet over moderate flame, include the onion and continue to cook it for five mins.

2. After adding the meat, continue to brown it for another five mins.

3. Place the other components in the bowl, give it a stir, cook it for half an hour across a moderate flame, then split it up and offer it.

Per serving: Calories: 280kcal; Protein: 21g; Carbs: 10g; Fat: 11g

62. Rosemary Chicken

Preparation time: ten mins

Cooking time: ten mins

Servings: two

Ingredients:

- Two zucchinis
- One carrot
- One teaspoon dried rosemary
- Four chicken breasts
- 1/2 bell pepper
- 1/2 red onion
- Eight garlic cloves
- Olive oil
- 1/4 tablespoon ground pepper

Directions:

1. Prepare the oven and preheat it at 375 °F (or 200°C).

2. Slice both zucchini and carrots and add bell pepper, onion, garlic, and put everything adding oil in a 13" x 9" pan.

3. Spread the pepper over everything and roast for around ten mins.

4. In the meantime, lift the chicken skin and spread black pepper and rosemary on the flesh.

5. Remove the vegetable pan from the microwave and include the chicken, returning it to the oven for about 30 more minutes. Serve and enjoy!

Per serving: Calories: 215kcal; Protein: 2g; Carbs: 4g; Fat: 6.3g

63. Pork Chops with Tomato Salsa

Preparation time: fifteen mins

Cooking time: fifteen mins

Servings: four

Ingredients:

- four pork chops
- one tbsp. olive oil

- four scallions, sliced
- one tsp. cumin, ground
- half tbsp. hot paprika
- one tsp. garlic powder
- tweak of sea salt
- tweak of black pepper
- one small red onion, sliced
- two tomatoes, chopped
- two tbsps. lime juice
- one jalapeno, sliced
- quarter cup cilantro, sliced
- one tbsp. lime juice

Directions:

1. Include the scallions to a pot that has the oil already in it and cook them for about five mins over moderate flame.

2. After adding the meat, cumin paprika, garlic powder, salt, and pepper, and giving the mixture a shake, cook the meat for five mins on every end and then split it among the dishes.

3. To offer, place the tomatoes and the rest of the components inside a container, whisk, and then split them across the plates that contain the pork chops.

Per serving: Calories: 313kcal; Protein: 19.2g; Carbs: 5.9g; Fat: 23.7g

64. Mustard Pork Mix

Preparation time: ten mins

Cooking time: thirty-five mins

Servings: four

Ingredients:

- two shallots, sliced

- one lb. pork stew meat, chopped
- two garlic cloves, crushed
- two tbsps. olive oil
- quarter cup Dijon mustard
- two tbsps. chives, sliced
- one tsp. cumin, ground
- one tsp. rosemary, dried
- tweak of sea salt
- tweak of black pepper

Directions:

1. Place the oil in a skillet and bring it up to a moderate-high flame. Include the shallots and cook them for five mins.

2. Place the meat in the pan, and continue to brown it for another five mins.

3. Whisk in the other components, then continue cooking over a moderate flame for another quarter of an hour.

4. Serve the mixture in individual portions.

Per serving: Calories: 280kcal; Protein: 17g; Carbs: 11.8g; Fat: 14.3g

65. Smokey Turkey Chili

Preparation time: 5 mins

Cooking time: 45 mins

Servings: 8

Ingredients:

- 12ounce lean ground turkey
- half red onion, chopped
- Two cloves garlic, crushed and chopped
- ½ teaspoon of smoked paprika
- ½ teaspoon of chili powder
- ½ teaspoon of dried thyme

- ¼ cup reduced-sodium beef stock
- ½ cup of water
- 1 ½ cups baby spinach leaves, washed
- Three wheat tortillas

Directions:

1. Brown the ground beef in a dry skillet over medium-high heat.

2. Add in the red onion and garlic.

3. Sauté the onion until it goes clear.

4. Toss everything in the skillet into the crock pot.

5. Put in the rest of the stuff and let it simmer on low for 3–5 minutes.

6. Stir through the spinach for the last few minutes to wilt.

7. Slice tortillas and gently toast under the broiler until slightly crispy.

8. Serve on top of the turkey chili.

Per serving: Calories: 93.5kcal; Protein: 8g; Carbs: 3g; Fat: 5.5g

66. Lamb with Prunes

Preparation time: 15 minutes

Cooking time: 2 to 3 hours

Servings: 4-6

Ingredients:

- Three tablespoons coconut oil
- Two onions, sliced finely
- one (one-inch) piece fresh ginger, crushed
- Three garlic cloves, crushed
- half tsp. ground turmeric
- 2 ½ pound lamb shoulder, trimmed and cubed into 3-inch size

- Salt and freshly ground black pepper
- ½ teaspoon saffron threads, crumbled
- One cinnamon stick
- 3 cups of water
- one cup prunes, eroded & shared

Directions:

1. Inside a big pot, dissolve coconut oil on moderate flame.

2. Include onions, ginger, garlic cloves, and turmeric and fry for about three to five mins.

3. Sprinkling the lamb with salt and black pepper evenly.

4. In the pan, add lamb and saffron threads and cook for approximately four to five mins.

5. Include cinnamon stick and water and produce to some boil on high heat.

6. Reduce the temperature to low and simmer, covered for around 1½-120 minutes or until the lamb's desired doneness.

7. Stir in prunes and simmer for approximately 20-a half-hour.

8. Remove cinnamon stick and serve hot.

Per serving: Calories: 393kcal; Protein: 36g; Carbs: 10g; Fat: 12g

67. Ground Chicken and Peas Curry

Preparation time: fifteen mins

Cooking time: 6 to 10 mins

Servings: 3-4

Ingredients:

- Three tbsps. essential olive oil
- Two bay leaves
- Two onions, ground to some paste
- ½ tablespoon garlic paste
- ½ tablespoon ginger paste
- Two tomatoes, chopped finely
- One tablespoon ground cumin
- One tablespoon ground coriander
- One tsp. ground turmeric
- One tsp. red chili powder
- Salt, as required
- one lb. lean ground chicken
- 2 cups frozen peas
- 1½ cups water
- 1-2 teaspoons garam masala powder

Directions:

1. Inside a deep griddle, heat oil on moderate flame.

2. Include bay leaves and fry for around ½ a min.

3. Include onion paste and fry for approximately three to four mins.

4. Saute the paste for about 1 minute and 15 seconds before adding the garlic and ginger.

5. Add tomatoes and spices and cook, occasionally stirring, for about 3-4 minutes.

6. Stir in chicken and cook for about 4-5 minutes.

7. Stir in peas and water and bring to a boil on high heat.

8. Reduce the heat to low and simmer approximately 5-8 minutes or till the anticipated doneness.

9. Mix in garam masala and eliminate from flame.

10. Serve warm.

Per serving: Calories: 450kcal; Protein: 38g; Carbs: 19g; Fat: 10g

68. Pork with Chili Zucchinis and Tomatoes

Preparation time: 15 mins

Cooking time: thirty-five mins

Servings: four

Ingredients:

- two tomatoes, chopped
- four scallions, sliced
- 3 tbsps. olive oil
- one zucchini, cut
- one lime juice
- two pounds pork stew meat, cubed
- two tbsps. chili powder
- half tbsps. cumin powder
- tweak of sea salt
- tweak black pepper

Directions:

1. Place the oil in a skillet and bring it up to a moderate-high flame. Include the shallots and cook them for five mins.

2. Place the meat in the pan, and continue to brown it for another five mins.

3. Whisk in the other components, then continue cooking over a moderate flame for another quarter of an hour.

Per serving: Calories: 300kcal; Protein: 14g; Carbs: 12g; Fat: 5g

69. Oregano Pork

Preparation time: 15 mins

Cooking time: eight hrs

Servings: four

Ingredients:

- two lbs. pork roast, cut
- two tbsps. oregano, sliced
- quarter cup balsamic vinegar
- one cup tomato paste
- one tbsp. sweet paprika
- one tsp. onion powder
- two tbsps. chili powder
- two garlic cloves, crushed
- A tweak of salt and black pepper

Directions:

1. Put the roast, oregano, vinegar, and the remaining components in the slow cooker, mix, cover, and cook on Low for 8 hours.

2. Divide everything between plates and serve.

Per serving: Calories: 300kcal; Protein: 24g; Carbs: 12g; Fat: 5g

70. Beef with Carrot & Broccoli

Preparation time: ten mins

Cooking time: fourteen mins

Servings: four

Ingredients:

- two tbsps. coconut oil, shared
- two average garlic cloves, crushed
- one pound beef sirloin steak, cut into fine strips
- Salt, as required
- quarter cup chicken broth
- two tsps. fresh ginger, aggravated
- one tablespoon Ground flax seeds
- half teaspoon Red pepper flakes, minced

- quarter teaspoon freshly ground black pepper
- one big carrot, skinned and cut finely
- two cups broccoli florets
- one average scallion, cut finely

Directions:

1. One tablespoon of oil should be heated in a griddle over moderate-high flame.

2. Place garlic and fry for around a min.

3. After adding the meat and the salt, continue to cook it for around four to five mins, or until it has browned.

4. The steak should be transferred into a container utilizing a slotted spatula.

5. Remove the liquid that's been sitting in the griddle.

6. Combine simultaneously inside a container the broth, the ginger, the flax seeds, the crushed red pepper, and the ground black pepper.

7. The rest of the oil should be heated up in the similar griddle over moderate flame.

8. Cook the carrot, broccoli, and ginger solution for around three to four mins, or until the vegetables have reached the doneness you prefer.

9. Cook for almost three to four mins after mixing in the beef and scallion.

Per serving: Calories: 412kcal; Protein: 35g; Carbs: 28g; Fat: 13g

71. Pork with Pears and Ginger

Preparation time: ten mins

Cooking time: thirty-five mins

Servings: four

Ingredients:

- two green onions, sliced
- two tbsps. avocado oil
- two lbs. pork roast, cut
- half cup coconut aminos
- one tbsp. ginger, crushed
- two pears, cored and sliced into pieces
- quarter cup vegetable stock
- one tbsp. chives, sliced

Directions:

1. Brown the beef for 2 minutes on each side, then add the onions and cook everything together for another 2 minutes over medium heat.

2. After adding the remaining components, give everything a light whisk, then bake it at 390 degrees Fahrenheit for half an hour.

3. After dividing the mixture among the dishes, serve the dish.

Per serving: Calories: 220kcal; Protein: 8g; Carbs: 16.5g; Fat: 13.3g

72. Turkey Sausages

Preparation time: 10 minutes

Cooking time: 10 minutes

Servings: 2

Ingredients:

- 1/4 teaspoon salt
- 1/8 teaspoon garlic powder
- 1/8 teaspoon onion powder
- One teaspoon fennel seed

• 1 pound 7%g; Fat: ground turkey

Directions:

1. Press the fennel seed and put together turkey with fennel seed, garlic, onion powder, and salt in a small cup.

2. Cover the bowl and refrigerate overnight.

3. Prepare the turkey with seasoning into different portions with a circle form and press them into patties ready to be cooked.

4. Cook at medium heat until browned.

5. Cook it for 1 to 2 minutes per side and serve them hot. Enjoy!

Per serving: Calories: 55kcal; Protein: 3g; Carbs: 5g; Fat: 7g

73. Pork Kabobs with Bell Peppers

Preparation time: 15 mins

Cooking time: 13 mins

Servings: four

Ingredients:

• 3 red bell peppers, sliced

• two lbs. pork, chopped

• one red onion, sliced

• one zucchini, cut

• Juice of one lime

• two tbsps. chili powder

• two tbsps. hot sauce

• half tbsp. cumin powder

• quarter cup olive oil

• quarter cup salsa

• tweak of sea salt

• tweak of black pepper

Directions:

1. Inside a bowl, all of the following ingredients are combined: salsa, lime juice, oil, hot sauce, chilli powder, cumin, salt, and black pepper.

2. Skewer the pork, bell peppers, zucchini, and onion, and afterwards brush them with the salsa after they are done.

3. Cook them for six mins on every end by placing them onto a grill that has been warmed up and then placing it across moderate-high flame.

4. Split among dishes and offer.

5. Relish!

Per serving: Calories: 300kcal; Protein: 14g; Carbs: 12g; Fat: 5g

74. Cranberry Pork

Preparation time: fifteen mins

Cooking time: eight hrs

Servings: four

Ingredients:

• one and a half lb. pork roast

• half tsp. fresh grated ginger

• two tbsps. coconut flour

• A tweak of mustard powder

• A tweak of salt and black pepper

• half cup cranberries

• quarter cup water

• Juice of half lemon

• two garlic cloves, crushed

Directions:

1. Place the roast in the slow cooker and stir in the ginger, flour, mustard, salt, and pepper. Next, add the cranberries, water, lemon juice,

and garlic. Cook, covered, on the lowest possible heat setting for around eight hrs. Cut all into bite-sized pieces, then distribute it evenly among the dishes, and offer.

2. Relish!

Per serving: Calories: 261kcal; Protein: 17g; Carbs: 9g; Fat: 4g

75. Pork and Leeks

Preparation time: ten mins

Cooking time: one hr & fifteen mins

Servings: four

Ingredients:

- two lbs. pork, chopped
- two carrots, sliced
- three leek, sliced
- one celery stalk, sliced
- one tsp. black peppercorns
- two yellow onions, sliced
- one tbsp. sliced parsley
- two cups coconut cream
- one tsp. mustard
- A tweak of salt and black pepper

Directions:

1. Place the meat in a pan and include enough water to seal it, along with the peppercorns, leeks, carrots, celery, and onions. Raise to a simmer across moderate flame, and then continue cooking for an additional hr while whisking frequently.

2. After stirring in the cream, mustard, salt, and pepper, continuing to cook the mixture for fifteen mins, dividing it among plates, and serving it with parsley on surface is recommended.

3. Relish!

Per serving: Calories: 250kcal; Protein: 18g; Carbs: 18g; Fat: 7g

CHAPTER 5
FISH

76. Wasabi Salmon Burgers

Preparation time: ten mins

Cooking time: 10 mins

Servings: 4

Ingredie

nts:

- ½ tsp. raw honey
- two tbsps. decreased-salt soy sauce
- one teaspoon wasabi powder
- one whisked free range egg
- two tins of wild salmon, wearied
- two scallions, sliced
- two tablespoons coconut oil
- one tablespoon fresh ginger, crushed

Directions:

1. Inside a container, combine the salmon, egg, ginger, scallions, and one tbsp. of oil together thoroughly using your hands, then shape the mixture into four patties.

2. toss the honey, wasabi powder, and soy sauce together inside a distinct dish till the ingredients are completely incorporated.

3. Cook the patties in a pot with one tbsp. of oil across moderate flame for four mins per end, or till the patties have reached the desired consistency and have browned.

4. Glaze the surface of every burger with the wasabi solution, then continue cooking the patties for further fifteen secs prior to serving.

5. If you want a healthier indulgence, serve it with your favourite side salad or some vegetables.

Per serving: Calories: 253kcal; Protein: 32g; Carbs: 3g; Fat: 13g

77. Beet Haddock Dinner

Preparation time: 10 minutes

Cooking time: 40-45 minutes

Servings: 4

Ingredients:

- 2 tablespoons olive oil
- 2 tablespoons apple cider vinegar
- 1 teaspoon chopped fresh thyme
- 8 beets, peeled and cut into small chunks
- 2 shallots, (cut into slices)
- 1 teaspoon minced garlic
- Pinch sea salt to taste
- 4 (5-ounce) haddock fillets, patted dry

Directions:

1. Preheat an oven to 400°F. Grease a baking dish with some cooking spray.

2. In a bowl (medium size), mix the beets, shallots, garlic, and 1 tablespoon olive oil.

3. Add the beet mixture in the baking dish.

4. Bake for about 25-30 mins, or till the vegetables are caramelized.

5. Eliminate from microwave and stir in the cider vinegar, thyme, and sea salt.

6. In a skillet (you can also use a saucepan); heat the remaining oil over moderate stove flame.

7. Include the fish, mix the solution and cook whilst whisking for 12-15 minutes until cooks well.

8. Flake the fish and serve with roasted beets.

Per serving: Calories: 324kcal; Protein: 37g; Carbs: 22g; Fat: 8g

78. Halibut Curry

Preparation time: ten mins

Cooking time: ten mins

Servings: four

Ingredients:

- two tablespoons additional-virgin olive oil
- two teaspoons ground turmeric
- two teaspoons curry powder
- one and a half pounds halibut, skin and bones eliminated, sliced into one-inch parts
- four cups no-salt-included chicken broth
- one (fourteen-ounce) tin lite coconut milk
- ½ teaspoon sea salt
- ¼ teaspoon newly ground black pepper

Directions:

1. Olive oil should be heated in a nonstick saucepan on moderate-high flame till it glistens before being added to the pan.

2. To this, include the curry powder and turmeric. To blossom the seasonings, continue cooking for another two mins while mixing continuously.

3. The halibut, chicken stock, coconut milk, black pepper, and salt should all be added at this point. Raise towards a boil, afterwards reduce the flame to keep it at a simmer for as long as possible.

4. Simmer for about seven mins, mixing once or twice during that time, till the salmon becomes transparent.

Per serving: Calories: 429kcal; Protein: 27g; Carbs: 5g; Fat: 47g

79. Honey Scallops

Preparation time: 5 mins

Cooking time: 25 mins

Servings: 4

Ingredients:

- one lb. large scallops, rinsed
- Dash of ground black pepper and salt to taste
- 3 tablespoons coconut aminos
- two garlic cloves, crushed
- two tbsps. avocado oil
- quarter cup raw honey
- one tablespoon apple cider vinegar

Directions:

1. The scallops should be salted and peppered.

2. In a skillet (you can also use a saucepan); heat the oil over moderate stove flame.

3. Include the scallops, mix the solution and cook whilst mixing for around two to three mins till tendered and golden.

4. Place in a plate, and put away.

5. In the identical skillet or pot, warm the honey, coconut aminos, garlic, and vinegar.

6. Cook for 6-7 minutes; add the scallops and coat well. Serve warm.

Per serving: Calories: 346kcal; Protein: 21g; Carbs: 27g; Fat: 17g

80. Garlic Cod Meal

Preparation time: 5 minutes

Cooking time: 35 minutes

Servings: 4

Ingredients:

- 2 tablespoons olive oil
- 2 tablespoons tarragon, chopped
- ¼ cup parsley, chopped
- 4 cod fillets, skinless
- 3 garlic cloves, minced
- 1 yellow onion, chopped
- (ground) black pepper and salt to the taste
- Juice of 1 lemon
- 1 lemon, (cut into slices)
- 1 tablespoon thyme, chopped
- 4 cups water

Directions:

1. Inside a skillet heat the oil over moderate stove flame.

2. Include the onions, garlic, mix the solution and cook whilst blending for almost two to three mins till tendered.

3. Add the salt, pepper, tarragon, parsley, thyme, water, lemon juice and lemon slices.

4. Boil the mix; add the cod, cook for 12-15 minutes, drain the liquid.

5. Serve with a side salad.

Per serving: Calories: 181kcal; Protein: 12g; Carbs: 9g; Fat: 3g

81. Citrus Salmon on a Bed of Greens

Preparation time: ten mins

Cooking time: nineteen mins

Servings: four

Ingredients:

- quarter cup additional-virgin olive oil, shared
- one and a half pounds (68g;) salmon
- one teaspoon sea salt, shared
- ½ teaspoon newly ground black pepper, shared
- Zest of 1 lemon
- 6 cups stemmed and chopped swiss chard
- 3 garlic cloves, minced
- Juice of 2 lemons

Directions:

1. Two tbsps. of the olive oil should be heated till they glistens in a saucepan that is nonstick and set across moderate-high flame.

2. A half tsp. of the salt, a quarter tsp. of the pepper, and the lemon juice should be used to season the salmon. After placing the salmon in the pan skin-side up, proceed to roast it for approximately seven mins, or till the flesh is transparent. After you have flipped the salmon, continue cooking it for another three to four mins. Place on a platter, tent-like from above with aluminium foil, and put away.

3. Place the saucepan back over the burner's heat source, include the two additional tbsps. of olive oil, and warm the oil till it glistens.

4. The Swiss chard should be added. Cook for approximately seven mins, swirling the mixture on occasion, till it is tender.

5. Mix in the minced garlic. Cook for another thirty secs while swirling all the time.

6. The rest of the quarter tsp. of pepper, the rest of the half tsp. of salt, and the lemon juice should be sprinkled in at this point. Prepare for two mins.

7. On top of the Swiss greens, serve the smoked salmon.

Per serving: Calories: 363kcal; Protein: 34g; Carbs: 3g; Fat: 25g

82. Salmon Ceviche

Preparation time: 10 minutes

Cooking time: 20 minutes

Servings: 4

Ingredients:

• 1 lb. salmon, skin & pin bones removed, cut into bite-size pieces (remove any gray flesh)
• ½ cup freshly embraced lime juice
• two tomatoes, chopped
• ¼ cup new cilantro leaves, sliced
• one jalapeño pepper, sowed & chopped
• two tablespoons additional-virgin olive oil
• ½ teaspoon sea salt

Directions:

1. Inside a moderate container, combine the lime juice and the salmon and toss to combine. Allow it to sit in the marinade for twenty mins.

2. Mix in the tomatoes, cilantro, jalapeo, olive oil, and salt until everything is well combined.

Per serving: Calories: 222kcal; Protein: 23g; Carbs: 3g; Fat: 14g

83. Miso-Glazed Salmon

Preparation time: 5 mins

Cooking time: ten mins

Servings: four

Ingredients:

• four (4-ounce / 113-g) salmon fillets
• 3 tablespoons miso paste

• 2 tablespoons raw honey
• 1 teaspoon coconut aminos
• 1 teaspoon rice vinegar

Directions:

1. Preheat the broiler.

2. Line a baking dish with aluminum foil and place the salmon fillets in it.

3. In a small bowl, stir together the miso, honey, coconut aminos, and vinegar. Glaze each fillet by brushing it with the glaze.

4. Broil for about 5 minutes. The fish is done when it flakes easily. The exact cooking time depends on its thickness.

5. Brush any remaining glaze over the fish, and continue to broil for 5 minutes, if needed.

Per serving: Calories: 264kcal; Protein: 30g; Carbs: 13g; Fat: 9g

84. Coconut Chili Salmon

Preparation time: 10 minutes

Cooking time: 25 minutes

Servings: 6

Ingredients:

• 1 ¼ cups coconut, shredded
• 2 tablespoons olive oil
• ¼ cup water
• 1 pound salmon, cubed
• 1/3 cup coconut flour
• A pinch of (ground) black pepper and salt
• 1 egg
• 4 red chilies, chopped
• 3 garlic cloves, minced
• ¼ cup balsamic vinegar

- ½ cup raw honey

Directions:

1. Inside a container (average sized), mix the flour using a pinch of salt.

2. In another bowl, whip the egg with the black pepper.

3. Add the shredded coconut in another bowl.

4. Coat the salmon cubes in flour, egg and coconut mix one by one.

5. In a skillet (you can also use a saucepan); heat the oil over medium stove flame.

6. Add the salmon, stir-fry them for 2-3 minutes on each side. Place in serving plates.

7. Heat water across moderate-high flame in the pan, include the chilies, cloves, vinegar and honey, stir gently.

8. Boil the mix and simmer for 4 minutes; top over the salmon and serve.

Per serving: Calories: 218kcal; Protein: 17g; Carbs: 14g; Fat: 5g

85. Vinegar Spiced Salmon with Honey

Preparation time: two mins

Cooking time: eight mins

Servings: four

Ingredients:

- half cup balsamic vinegar
- 1 tbsp. honey
- four (eight-oz. / 227-gram) salmon fillets
- Sea salt and freshly ground pepper, to taste
- one tbsp. olive oil

Directions:

1. Bring a griddle up to a temperature of moderate-high. In a low-volume dish, mix the honey and vinegar together.

2. Salt and freshly ground black pepper should be used to top the salmon fillets before they are brushed with the honey-balsamic sauce.

3. Cook the salmon fillets for about 3–4 minutes each side, or till mildly browned and average rare in the middle, in a pan coated with olive oil.

4. Allow it to stay idle for five mins prior to offering.

Per serving: Calories: 454kcal; Protein: 65g; Carbs: 9.7g; Fat: 17g

86. Fennel Baked Cod

Preparation time: ten mins

Cooking time: 25 mins

Servings: four

Ingredients:

- 3 sun-dried tomatoes, chopped
- 1 small red onion, (cut into slices)
- ½ fennel bulb, (cut into slices)
- 2 cod fillets, boneless
- 1 garlic clove, minced
- 1 teaspoon olive oil
- Black pepper to the taste
- 4 black olives, pitted and sliced
- 2 rosemary springs
- ¼ teaspoon red pepper flakes

Directions:

1. Warm up a microwave to 400°F. Spray some cooking spray in a baking dish.

2. Add the cod, garlic, black pepper, tomatoes, onion, fennel, olives, rosemary and pepper flakes; mix gently.

3. Bake for 14-15 mins.

4. Split the fish solution among dishes & offer.

Per serving: Calories: 255kcal; Protein: 16g; Carbs: 11g; Fat: 4g

87. Ginger and Chili Sea Bass Fillets

Preparation time: 10 mins

Cooking time: ten mins

Servings: two

Ingredients:

- two sea bass fillets
- one teaspoon black pepper
- one tablespoon additional-virgin olive oil
- one teaspoon ginger, skinned & sliced
- one garlic clove, finely sliced
- one red chili, deseeded and finely cut
- two green onion stems, sliced

Directions:

1. Obtain a pan and place it over a flame source that ranges from moderate to high. Warm the oil.

2. The sea bass should be seasoned with black pepper, and the skin should be scored on several occasions with a pointed knife before cooking.

3. Place the skin side down of the sea bass fillet into the heated pan.

4. Cook for five mins before turning the meat over.

5. Continue to cook for an additional two mins.

6. Take the sea bass out of the pan.

7. After adding the chili, garlic, and ginger, continue to simmer for about two mins, or till the garlic and ginger become golden.

8. Take the dish off the flame and then stir in the green scallions.

9. When you're ready to offer the sea bass, spread the vegetables across the top.

Per serving: Calories: 204kcal; Protein: 25g; Carbs: 4g; Fat: 10g

88. Herbed Mussels Treat

Preparation time: 5 minutes

Cooking time: 30 minutes

Servings: 4

Ingredients:

- 1 tablespoon olive oil
- 2 teaspoons minced garlic
- 1 cup coconut milk
- ½ cup chicken bone broth
- two tsps. sliced fresh thyme
- one tsp. sliced fresh oregano
- one and a half pounds mussels, scrubbed and debearded
- 1 scallion, sliced white and green parts

Directions:

1. Inside a skillet (you could further utilize a pot); heat the oil over moderate stove flame.

2. After adding the garlic, mix the solution and continue to simmer whilst mixing for approximately two to three mins, or till the garlic has tendered.

3. Add the coconut milk, broth, thyme, and oregano.

4. Boil the mix and add the mussels. Cover and cook for about 8 minutes, or until the shells opened up.

5. Remove any unopened shells and add in the scallion; serve warm.

Per serving: Calories: 318kcal; Protein: 23g; Carbs: 12g; Fat: 21g

89. Fresh Tuna Steak and Fennel Salad

Preparation time: fifteen mins

Cooking time: 25 mins

Servings: four

Ingredients:

• two (1 inch) tuna steaks

• 2 tablespoons olive oil, 1 tablespoon olive oil for brushing

• 1 teaspoon crushed black peppercorns

• 1 teaspoon crushed fennel seeds

• 1 fennel bulb, trimmed and sliced

• ½ cup water

• 1 lemon, juiced

• 1 teaspoon fresh parsley, chopped

Directions:

1. Coat the fish using oil and afterwards top via peppercorns and fennel seeds.

2. Warm up the oil on a moderate flame and fry the fennel bulb slices for 5 mins or till light brown.

3. Include the water to the pan and cook for 10 mins till fennel is softer.

4. Mix in the lemon juice and lower heat to a simmer.

5. Meanwhile, heat another skillet and sauté the tuna steaks for about 2 to 3 minutes each side for medium-rare.

6. Serve the fennel mix with the tuna steaks on top and garnish with the fresh parsley.

Per serving: Calories: 288kcal; Protein: 44g; Carbs: 6g; Fat: 9g

90. Orange and Maple-Glazed Salmon

Preparation time: fifteen mins

Cooking time: fifteen mins

Servings: four

Ingredients:

• Juice of 2 oranges

• Zest of one orange

• quarter cup pure maple syrup

• two tablespoons low-sodium soy sauce

• one teaspoon garlic powder

• four (four- to six-ounce / 113- to 170-g) salmon fillets, pin bones eliminated

Directions:

1. Turn the microwave temperature as high as 400° (2050C).

2. Mix the orange juice and zest, maple syrup, soy sauce, and garlic powder together inside a shallow container that is not very large.

3. Place the salmon chunks in the dish with the fleshy end facing below. Allow it to sit in the marinade for ten mins.

4. Bake the salmon for approximately fifteen mins, or till the interior is transparent, after which you ought to move it to a baking tray with a rim.

Per serving: Calories: 297kcal; Protein: 34g; Carbs: 18g; Fat: 11g

---

91. Kale Cod Secret

Preparation time: 10 minutes

Cooking time: 30 minutes

Servings: 4

Ingredients:

- 4 cod fillets, skinless and boneless
- 1 tablespoon ginger, (shredded or grated)
- 4 teaspoons lemon zest
- A pinch of (ground) black pepper and salt
- 3 leeks, chopped
- 2 cups veggie stock
- two tbsps. lemon juice
- two tbsps. olive oil
- one pound kale, chopped
- ½ teaspoon sesame oil

Directions:

1. Inside a container (moderate sized), mix the zest with salt and pepper. Coat the fish with this mix.

2. In a skillet (you can also use a saucepan); heat the leeks, ginger and lemon juice over medium stove flame.

3. Heat for a few minutes; include the fish fillets.

4. Cover and cook for 8-10 mins, transfer it to a plate.

5. Strain the liquid and reserve the leeks. Add the fish in serving plates.

6. In a skillet (you can also use a saucepan); heat the oil over moderate stove flame.

7. Include the kale, whisk the solution and cook whilst mixing for around 3-4 mins till tendered.

8. Add the soup liquid and cook for 4-5 minutes more.

9. Add the reserved leeks; cook for 2 minutes.

10. Divide into fish bowls, drizzle the sesame oil all over and serve.

Per serving: Calories: 238kcal; Protein: 16g; Carbs: 12g; Fat: 3g

---

92. Grilled Salmon Packets with Asparagus

Preparation time: fifteen mins

Cooking time: twenty mins

Servings: four

Ingredients:

- 4 (4-ounce / 113-g) skinless salmon fillets
- 16 asparagus spears, tough ends trimmed
- 4 tablespoons avocado oil, divided
- one tsp. garlic powder, divided
- ½ tsp. salt, divided
- Newly ground black pepper, to taste
- 1 lemon, thinly sliced

Directions:

1. Preheat the oven to 400 degrees (205°C).

2. Cut 4 (12-inch) squares of parchment paper or foil and put on a work surface.

3. Place 1 salmon fillet in the center of each square and 4 asparagus spears next to each fillet. Brush the fish and asparagus with 1 tablespoon of avocado oil.

4. Sprinkle each fillet with ¼ teaspoon garlic powder and 1teaspoon salt, and season with pepper. Place the lemon slices on top of the

fillets. Close and seal the parchment around each fillet so it forms a sealed packet. Put the parchment packets onto a baking tray. Bake for 20 minutes.

5. Place a sealed parchment packet on each of 4 plates and serve hot.

Per serving: Calories: 339kcal; Protein: 30g; Carbs: 1g; Fat: 23g

93. Scrumptious Coconut Shrimps

Preparation time: five mins

Cooking time: fifteen to twenty mins

Servings: 4

Ingredients:

- two eggs
- one cup dried shredded coconut, unsweetened
- ¼ teaspoon paprika
- Dash cayenne pepper
- ¼ cup coconut flour
- ½ teaspoon salt
- Dash freshly grounds black pepper
- ¼ cup coconut oil
- 1-pound raw shrimp, peeled and deveined

Directions:

1. In a bowl, whisk the eggs.

2. In another bowl, mix the coconut, flour, salt, paprika, cayenne pepper, and black pepper.

3. Coat the shrimp into the egg mixture, and then into the coconut mix.

4. In a skillet (you can also use a saucepan); heat the oil over medium stove flame.

5. Add the shrimps and cook for 2-3 minutes per side. Serve warm.

Per serving: Calories: 246kcal; Protein: 19g; Carbs: 8g; Fat: 18g

94. Lime-Salmon Patties

Preparation time: 20 mins

Cooking time: 10 mins

Servings: four

Ingredients:

- ½ pound (22g;) cooked boneless salmon fillet, flaked
- 2 eggs
- ¾ cup almond flour, plus more as needed
- 1 scallion, white and green parts, chopped
- Juice of 2 limes (2 to 4 tablespoons), plus more as needed
- Zest of 2 limes (optional)
- 1 tablespoon chopped fresh dill
- Pinch sea salt
- 1 tablespoon olive oil
- 1 lime, cut into wedges

Directions:

1. In a large bowl, mix together the salmon, eggs, almond flour, scallion, lime juice, lime zest (if using), dill, and sea salt until the mixture holds together when pressed. If the mixture is too dry, add more lime juice; if it is too wet, add more almond flour.

2. Divide the salmon mixture into 4 equal portions, and press them into patties about ½ inch thick. Refrigerate them for about 30 minutes to firm up.

3. Put a big skillet over moderate-high flame and include the olive oil.

4. Add the salmon patties and brown for around five mins on each end, turning once. 5. Serve the patties with lime wedges.

Per serving: Calories: 243kcal; Protein: 18g; Carbs: 5g; Fat: 18g

---

95. Salmon Broccoli Bowl

Preparation time: 5 minutes

Cooking time: 20 minutes

Servings: 4

Ingredients:

- 3 tablespoons avocado oil
- 2 garlic cloves, minced
- 1 broccoli head, separate florets
- 1 ½ pounds salmon fillets, boneless
- A pinch of (ground) black pepper and salt
- Juice of ½ lemon

Directions:

1. Preheat an oven to 450°F. Line a baking sheet with a foil.

2. Spread the broccoli; add the salmon, oil, garlic, salt, pepper and the lemon juice, toss gently.

3. Bake for 15 minutes.

4. Divide in serving plates and serve warm.

Per serving: Calories: 207kcal; Protein: 9g; Carbs: 14g; Fat: 6g

CHAPTER 6
VEGETABLES

96. Onion and Orange Healthy Salad

Preparation time: 15 mins

Cooking time: zero mins

Servings: three

Ingredients:

- 8 big orange
- 4 tbsps. red wine vinegar
- 8 tbsps. olive oil
- one tsp. dried oregano
- one red onion, finely cut
- one cup olive oil
- quarter cup of fresh chives, sliced
- Ground black pepper

Directions:

1. After peeling the orange, divide it into quarters and then every quarter into four to five diagonal pieces.

2. Put the oranges in a wide, shallow bowl.

3. Sprinkle with vinegar, then add olive oil and oregano.

4. Whisk.

5. Chill for thirty mins.

6. Distribute cut onion and black olives on surface.

7. To finish, garnish with a few extra scallions and a generous amount of freshly ground black pepper.

8. Serve, and have fun with it!

Per serving: Calories: 120kcal; Protein: 2g; Carbs: 20g; Fat: 6g

97. Turmeric Endives

Preparation time: ten mins

Cooking time: 20 mins

Servings: four

Ingredients:

- two endives, shared lengthwise
- two tbsps. olive oil
- one tsp. rosemary, dried
- half tsp. turmeric powder
- A tweak of black pepper

Directions:

1. Combine the endives alongside the oil and the other ingredients in a baking pan, toss gently, bake at 400 degrees F within 20 minutes.

2. Serve as a side dish.

Per serving: Calories: 64kcal; Protein: 0.2g; Carbs: 0.8g; Fat: 7.1g

98. Curried Okra

Preparation time: ten mins

Cooking time: twelve mins

Servings: four

Ingredients:

- one pound small to average okra pods, clipped
- quarter teaspoon curry powder
- half teaspoon kosher salt
- one teaspoon thinly sliced serrano chili
- one teaspoon ground coriander
- one tablespoon canola oil
- three-quarter teaspoon brown mustard seeds

Direction:

1. Put a big and solid griddle over a temperature that is moderate-high, and sauté the mustard seeds till aromatic, which should take almost thirty secs.

2. Include canola oil. Include okra in the dish along with curry powder, salt, pepper, and ground coriander. Whisk the mixture occasionally whilst cooking it for one min inside a fry pan.

3. Place a seal on the pan and continue to simmer across a low flame for around eight mins. Mix it up every so often.

4. Remove the cover, raise the heat to moderate-high, and continue cooking the okra for about two additional mins, or till it has a light brown colour.

5. Offer, and have fun with it!

Per serving: Calories: 78kcal; Protein: 2g; Carbs: 6g; Fat: 6g

99. Roasted Portobellos With Rosemary

Preparation time: 10 mins

Cooking time: fifteen mins

Servings: four

Ingredients:

- 10 portobello mushroom, clipped
- one sprig rosemary, ragged
- two tbsps. fresh lemon juice
- quarter cup additional virgin olive oil
- one clove garlic, crushed
- Salt and pepper, as required

Directions:

1. The microwave should be preheated to 450°F.

2. Use a container and include the entire components.

3. Whisk to cover.

4. Put the mushroom inside a baking tray stem side up.

5. Roast in the microwave for fifteen mins.

6. Offer and relish!

Per serving: Calories: 63kcal; Protein: 1g; Carbs: 2g; Fat: 6g

100. Cauliflower Hash Brown

Preparation time: ten mins

Cooking time: twenty mins

Servings: six

Ingredients:

- four eggs, whisked
- half cup coconut milk
- half tsp. dry mustard
- Salt and pepper, as required
- one big head cauliflower, ragged

Directions:

1. Put the entire components inside a blending dish and give it a good stir till everything is evenly distributed.

2. Prepare a frypan that doesn't adhere and warm it across a moderate flame.

3. The cauliflower solution should be added to the griddle inside a big dollop.

4. Fry each end for three mins, then toss and cook the subsequent end for one min, like you would with a pancake. Proceed with the rest of the components in the same manner.

5. Serve, and have fun with it!

Per serving: Calories: 102kcal; Protein: 5g; Carbs: 4g; Fat: 8g

101. Braised Kale

Preparation time: ten mins

Cooking time: fifteen mins

Servings: three

Ingredients:

- two-three tbsps. water
- one tablespoon coconut oil
- half cut red pepper
- two stalk celery (cut to quarter-inch dense)
- five cups of sliced kale

Directions:

1. Prepare a dish by heating a skillet across moderate flame.

2. After adding the coconut oil, cook the celery for around five mins while stirring frequently.

3. Include the greens and the red pepper in the dish.

4. Include one teaspoonful of water in the recipe.

5. The vegetables should be allowed to shrivel for a couple of mins. If the kale begins to adhere to the pot, include one tbsp. of water to the mixture.

6. To be served hot.

Per serving: Calories: 61kcal; Protein: 1g; Carbs: 3g; Fat: 5g

102. Sweet Potato Puree

Preparation time: ten mins

Cooking time: fifteen mins

Servings: five

Ingredients:

- two lbs. sweet potatoes, skinned
- one and a half cups water
- five Medjool dates, eroded & sliced

Directions:

1. Put the potatoes and the water into the saucepan.

2. Put the cover back on the saucepan and bring the water to a simmer. Boil the potatoes for around fifteen mins, or till they are tender.

3. After draining the potatoes, put them inside a mixing bowl along with the dates. Blend until smooth.

4. Process in a blender till completely homogeneous.

5. Serve, and have fun with it!

Per serving: Calories: 172kcal; Protein: 3g; Carbs: 41g; Fat: 0.2g

103. Spicy Wasabi Mayonnaise

Preparation time: fifteen mins

Cooking time: zero mins

Servings: four

Ingredients:

- half tbsp. wasabi paste
- one cup mayonnaise

Directions:

1. Put the wasabi paste and mayonnaise in a container and stir them together.

2. Combine thoroughly.

3. Allow it to refrigerate, and utilize it as required.

4. Offer, and have fun with it!

Per serving: Calories: 388kcal; Protein: 1g; Carbs: 1g; Fat: 42g

104. Spicy Veggie Pancakes

Preparation time: 20 minutes

Cooking time: 10 minutes

Servings: 4

Ingredients:

- Three tablespoons olive oil, divided
- Two small onions, finely chopped
- One jalapeño pepper, minced
- ¾ cup carrot, grated
- ¾ cup cabbage, finely chopped
- 1½ cups quick-cooking oats
- ¾ cup cooked brown rice
- ¾ cup of water
- ½ cup whole-wheat flour
- One large egg
- One large egg white
- One teaspoon baking soda
- ¼ teaspoon cayenne pepper

Directions:

1. Heat 2 teaspoons oil in a medium skillet over medium temperature.

2. Sauté the onion, jalapeño, carrot, and cabbage for 4 minutes.

3. While the veggies are cooking, combine the oats, rice, water, flour, egg, egg white, baking soda, and cayenne pepper in a medium bowl until well mixed.

4. Add the cooked vegetables to the mixture and stir to combine.

5. Heat the remaining oil in a huge skillet over medium heat.

6. Drop the mixture into the skillet, about 1/3 cup per pancake. Cook for four mins, or till bubbles form on the pancakes' surface and the edges look cooked, then carefully flip them over.

7. Cook the other side for 3 to 5 minutes or until the pancakes are hot and firm.

8. Replicate with the rest of the solution and offer.

Per serving: Calories: 323kcal; Protein: 10g; Carbs: 48g; Fat: 11g

105. Black-Eyed Peas and Greens Power Salad

Preparation time: 15 minutes

Cooking time: 6 minutes

Servings: 2

Ingredients:

- 1 tablespoon olive oil
- 3 cups purple cabbage, chopped
- 5 cups baby spinach
- 1 cup shredded carrots
- 1 can black-eyed peas, drained
- Juice of ½ lemon
- Salt
- Freshly ground black pepper

Directions:

1. In a medium pan, add the oil and cabbage and sauté for 1 to 2 minutes on medium heat. Add in your spinach, cover for 3 to 4 minutes on medium heat, until greens are wilted. Remove from the heat and add to a large bowl.

2. Add in the carrots, black-eyed peas, and a splash of lemon juice. Season with salt and pepper, if desired. Toss and serve.

Per serving: Calories: 320kcal; Protein: 16g; Carbs: 49g; Fat: 9g

106. Mushroom Tacos

Preparation time: ten mins

Cooking time: fifteen mins

Servings: 6

Ingredients:

• Six collard greens leave

• 2 cups mushrooms, chopped

• One white onion, chopped

• One tbsp. Taco seasoning

• One tablespoon coconut oil

• ½ tsp. salt

• ¼ cup fresh parsley

• One tablespoon mayonnaise

Directions:

1. Put the coconut oil in the skillet and melt it.

2. Add chopped mushrooms and diced onion. Mix up the ingredients.

3. Seal the cover and cook them for 10 mins.

4. After this, drizzle the vegetables with Taco seasoning, salt, and add fresh parsley.

5. Blend the mixture and cook for five mins more.

6. Now, include mayonnaise and stir well.

7. Chill the mushroom mixture a little.

8. Fill the collard green leaves with the mushroom mixture and fold up them.

Per serving: Calories: 52kcal; Protein: 1.4g; Carbs: 5.1g; Fat: 3.3g

107. Cauliflower Mashed Potatoes

Preparation time: ten mins

Cooking time: 10 mins

Servings: four

Ingredients:

• 16 cups water (enough to cover cauliflower)

• 1 head cauliflower (about 3 pounds), trimmed and cut into florets

• 4 garlic cloves

• 1 tablespoon olive oil

• quarter tsp. salt

• one-eighth tsp. newly ground black pepper

• 2 teaspoons dried parsley

Directions:

1. Boil a large pot of water, then the cauliflower and garlic. Cook within 10 minutes, then strain. Move it back to the hot pan, and let it stand within 2 to 3 minutes with the lid on.

2. Put the cauliflower plus garlic in a food processor or blender. Add the olive oil, salt, pepper, and purée until smooth. Taste and adjust the salt and pepper.

3. Remove, then put the parsley, and mix until combined. Garnish with additional olive oil, if desired. Serve immediately.

Per serving: Calories: 87kcal; Protein: 4g; Carbs: 12g; Fat: 4g

108. Stir-Fried Squash

Preparation time: ten mins

Cooking time: ten mins

Servings: four

Ingredients:

- one tbsp. olive oil
- three cloves of garlic, crushed
- one butternut squash, sowed & cut
- one tbsp. coconut aminos
- one tbsp. lemon juice
- one tbsp. water
- Salt and pepper, as required

Directions:

1. While the oil is heating, fry the garlic across a moderate temperature till it becomes perfumed.

2. After stirring in the zucchini for the first three mins, include the remaining components and mix to combine.

3. Put the cover back on the pot, and continue to boil the squash for another five mins, or till it reaches the desired consistency.

4. Offer, and have fun with it!

Per serving: Calories: 83kcal; Protein: 2g; Carbs: 14g; Fat: 3g

109. Zucchini Noodles with Spring Vegetables

Preparation time: 20 minutes

Cooking time: 10 minutes

Servings: 6

Ingredients:

- Six zucchinis, cut into long noodles
- 1 cup of halved snow peas
- 1 cup (3-inch pieces) of asparagus
- One tablespoon of olive oil
- One teaspoon of minced fresh garlic
- One tablespoon of newly clasped lemon juice
- one cup of shredded fresh spinach
- ¾ cup of halved cherry tomatoes
- Two tablespoons of sliced fresh basil leaves

Directions:

1. Fill an average pan with water, place over medium-high heat, and bring to a boil.

2. Reduce the heat to medium, and blanch the zucchini ribbons, snow peas, and asparagus by submerging them in the water for 1 minute. Drain and rinse immediately under cold water.

3. Pat the vegetables dry with paper towels and transfer to a large bowl.

4. Place an average skillet over medium heat, and increase the olive oil. Add the garlic, and sauté until tender, about 3 minutes.

5. Add the lemon juice and spinach, and sauté until the spinach is wilted, about 3 minutes.

6. Add the zucchini mixture, the cherry tomatoes, and basil and toss until well combined.

7. Serve immediately.

Per serving: Calories: 52kcal; Protein: 2g; Carbs: 4g; Fat: 2g

110. Lime Spinach and Chickpeas Salad

Preparation time: ten mins

Cooking time: zero mins

Servings: four

Ingredients:

- sixteen oz. tinned chickpeas, wearied & washed
- two cups baby spinach leaves

- half tbsp. lime juice
- Two tbsps. olive oil
- One tsp. cumin, ground
- A tweak of sea salt and black pepper
- half tsp. chili flakes

Directions:

1. In a bowl, combine chickpeas alongside the spinach and the remaining components, toss and serve cold.

Per serving: Calories: 240kcal; Protein: 12g; Carbs: 11.6g; Fat: 8.2g

111. Paprika Brussels Sprouts

Preparation time: 10 minutes

Cooking time: 25 minutes

Servings: 4

Ingredients:

- 2 tablespoons olive oil
- 1-pound Brussels sprouts, trimmed and halved
- 3 green onions, chopped
- 2 garlic cloves, minced
- 1 tablespoon balsamic vinegar
- 1 tablespoon sweet paprika
- A tweak of black pepper

Directions:

1. Bake the Brussels sprouts at 400°F for twenty-five mins after combining them inside a baking pot with the oil and the remaining components, then tossing the mixture.

2. After dividing the mixture among the dishes, offer the dish.

Per serving: Calories: 121kcal; Protein: 4.4g; Carbs: 12.6g; Fat: 7.6g

112. Vegetable Potpie

Preparation time: ten mins

Cooking time: ten mins

Servings: eight

Ingredients:

- one recipe pastry for double-crust pie
- two tbsps. cornstarch
- one teaspoon ground black pepper
- one teaspoon kosher salt
- three cups vegetable broth
- one cup fresh green beans, cracked into half inch
- two cups cauliflower florets
- two stalks celery, cut quarter inch wide
- two potatoes, skinned & chopped
- two big carrots, chopped
- one clove garlic, crushed
- eight ounces mushroom
- one onion, sliced
- two tbsps. olive oil

Directions:

1. Inside a big pot, fry the garlic in the oil till it is just beginning to turn golden. Include the onions and maintain frying till the onions are translucent and tender.

2. Fry the celery, potatoes, and carrots for three mins after adding them to the pan.

3. Raise to a boil the vegetable stock, green beans, and cauliflower that you have just added.

Slow heat and simmer till vegetables are mildly softer. Add some black pepper and salt to taste.

4. Cornstarch and a quarter cup of water should be combined in a small dish. Whisk the ingredients together till there are no longer any lumps in the concoction. After that, transfer the mixture into the pan containing the vegetables whilst continuously stirring.

5. Keep stirring for about three mins, or till the broth reaches the desired consistency. Take away from the flames.

6. In the meantime, roll out the pastry dough and position it on a baking dish that can go in the microwave measuring eleven by seven. After that, seal it with an additional layer of pastry dough and pour the vegetable mixture on top. Seal and flute the sides of the dough, then use a fork to make numerous pricks in the top dough and move on to the next step.

7. Cook the casserole in a microwave that has been warmed up to 425 degrees Fahrenheit for thirty mins, or till the crust has transformed a golden brown colour.

Per serving: Calories: 202kcal; Protein: 4g; Carbs: 26g; Fat: 10g

113. Cilantro And Avocado Platter

Preparation time: ten mins

Cooking time: zero mins

Servings: six

Ingredients:

- two avocados, skinned, eroded & chopped
- one sweet onion, sliced
- one green bell pepper, sliced
- one big ripe tomato, sliced
- quarter cup of fresh cilantro, sliced
- half a lime, juiced
- Salt and pepper, as required

Directions:

1. Put the onion, bell pepper, tomato, avocados, lime, and cilantro in a dish that's about the dimensions of a moderate container.

2. Provide it a good stir, then move it around.

3. Add some salt and pepper to flavor, and top it using salt and pepper.

4. Offer, and have fun with it!

Per serving: Calories: 126kcal; Protein: 2g; Carbs: 10g; Fat: 10g

114. Broccoli with Garlic and Lemon

Preparation time: 2 minutes

Cooking time: 4 minutes

Servings: 4

Ingredients:

- 1 cup of water
- 4 cups broccoli florets
- 1 teaspoon olive oil
- one tbsp. crushed garlic
- 1 tsp. lemon zest
- Salt
- Newly ground black pepper

Directions:

1. Put the broccoli in the boiling water in a small saucepan and cook within 2 to 3 minutes. The broccoli should retain its bright-green color. Drain the water from the broccoli.

2. Place the olive oil inside a small fry pot and turn the flame up to moderate-high. After adding the garlic, continue cooking for another thirty secs. Place the broccoli in the dish along with the lemon zest, salt, and pepper. After thoroughly combining, offer.

Per serving: Calories: 38kcal; Protein: 3g; Carbs: 5g; Fat: 1g

115. Stir-Fried Almond And Spinach

Preparation time: ten mins

Cooking time: fifteen mins

Servings: two

Ingredients:

- thirty-four lbs. spinach
- three tbsps. almonds
- Salt, as required
- one tbsp. coconut oil

Directions:

1. Put the oil in a big saucepan, then set it over a high flame setting.

2. After adding the spinach, continue to allow it to cook while mixing it periodically.

3. When the spinach is done cooking and has reached the desired tenderness, top it using salt and mix it.

4. Include almonds and relish!

Per serving: Calories: 150kcal; Protein: 8g; Carbs: 10g; Fat: 12g

CHAPTER 7 SIDES

116. Roasted Carrots

Preparation time: ten mins

Cooking time: forty mins

Servings: four

Ingredients:

- one onion, skinned and sliced
- eight carrots, skinned and sliced
- one tsp. thyme, sliced
- two tbsps. of additional-virgin olive oil
- half tsp. rosemary, sliced
- quarter tsp. ground pepper
- half tsp. salt

Directions:

1. Turn your microwave's temperature up to 425°Fahrenheit.

2. Whisk the onions, carrots, rosemary, thyme, pepper, and salt together in a basin before mixing in the remaining ingredients. Disperse out on the cookie tray you have.

3. Roast for forty mins. Onions and carrots ought to be browned and cooked through at this point.

Per serving: Calories: 126kcal; Protein: 2g; Carbs: 16g; Fat: 6g

117. Tomato Bulgur

Preparation time: seven mins

Cooking time: twenty mins

Servings: two

Ingredients:

- half cup bulgur
- one tsp. tomato paste
- half white onion, chopped
- two tbsps. coconut oil
- one and a half cup chicken stock

Directions:

1. Put some coconut oil in the frying pot and allow it to dissolve.

2. Roast the onion, after adding the chopped onion, till it is a light brown colour.

3. Now, include bulgur and mix thoroughly.

4. Cook the bulgur for three mins in the coconut oil.

5. After that, include the tomato paste while thoroughly combining the bulgur.

6. Include chicken stock.

7. Cook the bulgur for five mins at a flame setting that is anywhere between low and moderate.

8. The liquid ought to be absorbed by the cooked bulgur.

Per serving: Calories: 257kcal; Protein: 5.2g; Carbs: 30.2g; Fat: 14.5g

118. Beet Hummus

Preparation time: five mins

Cooking time: zero mins

Servings: two

Ingredients:

- one clove of garlic
- one skinless roasted beet
- one and three-quarter cup of chickpeas
- half cup olive oil
- two tbsps. sunflower seeds

- one lemon juice
- quarter teaspoon of chili flakes
- one and a half teaspoons of cumin
- one teaspoon of curry
- one teaspoon of maple syrup
- half teaspoon oregano
- half teaspoon salt
- one nub of fresh ginger

Directions:

1. Inside a mixing bowl, combine the entire components and mix them till they are completely uniform. Sprinkle some sunflower seeds on top before serving.

2. Relish!

Per serving: Calories: 423kcal; Protein: 13.9g; Carbs: 40.1g; Fat: 24.2g

119. Balsamic Cabbage

Preparation time: 10 minutes

Cooking time: 20 minutes

Servings: 4

Ingredients:

- 1-pound green cabbage, roughly shredded
- 2 tablespoons olive oil
- A pinch of black pepper
- 1 shallot, chopped
- 2 garlic cloves, minced
- 2 tablespoons balsamic vinegar
- 2 teaspoons hot paprika
- 1 teaspoon sesame seeds

Directions:

1. To prepare the shallot and garlic, warm the oil inside a skillet across moderate flame, include the shallot, and then fry the mixture for five mins.

2. After adding the cabbage and the remaining components, give everything a good whisk, then continue to prepare it across a flame setting of moderate for fifteen mins.

Per serving: Calories: 100kcal; Protein: 1.8g; Carbs: 8.2g; Fat: 7.5g

120. Chili Broccoli

Preparation time: ten mins

Cooking time: 30 mins

Servings: four

Ingredients:

- two tablespoons olive oil
- one pound broccoli florets
- two garlic cloves, crushed
- 2 tablespoons chili sauce
- 1 tablespoon lemon juice
- A pinch of black pepper
- 2 tablespoons cilantro, sliced

Directions:

1. Mix the broccoli, oil, garlic, and the remaining ingredients inside a baking pot, give the mixture a little whisk, and bake it at 400 degrees Fahrenheit for thirty mins.

2. Split the mix among dishes and offer as a side dish.

Per serving: Calories: 103kcal; Protein: 3.4g; Carbs: 8.3g; Fat: 7.4g

121. Lime Carrots

Preparation time: 10 mins

Cooking time: thirty mins

Servings: four

Ingredients:

- one pound baby carrots, trimmed
- one tbsp. sweet paprika
- 1 teaspoon lime juice
- 3 tablespoons olive oil
- A pinch of black pepper
- 1 teaspoon sesame seeds

Directions:

1. Arrange the carrots on a lined baking sheet, add the paprika and the other ingredients except for the sesame seeds, toss, bake at 400 ⁰F within 30 mins.

2. Split the carrots among dishes, drizzle sesame seeds on surface and offer as a side dish.

Per serving: Calories: 139kcal; Protein: 1.1g; Carbs: 10.5g; Fat: 11.2g

122. Lima Beans Dish

Preparation time: 10 minutes

Cooking time: 5 hours

Servings: 10

Ingredients:

- 1 green bell pepper, chopped
- 1 sweet red pepper, chopped
- 1 and ½ cups tomato sauce, salt-free
- 1 yellow onion, chopped
- ½ cup of water
- 16 ounces canned kidney beans, no-salt-added, drained and rinsed
- 16 ounces canned black-eyed peas, no-salt-added, drained and rinsed
- 15 ounces corn

- 15 ounces canned lima beans, no-salt-added, drained and rinsed
- 15 oz canned black beans, no-salt-added, drained
- 2 celery ribs, chopped
- 2 bay leaves
- 1 teaspoon ground mustard
- 1 tablespoon cider vinegar

Directions:

1. In your slow cooker, mix the tomato sauce with the celery, onion, green bell pepper, water, red pepper bay leaves, vinegar, mustard, kidney beans, corn, black-eyed peas, lima beans, and black beans, cook on Low within 5 hours.

2. Discard bay leaves, divide the whole mix between plates, and serve.

Per serving: Calories: 602kcal; Protein: 33g; Carbs: 117.7g; Fat: 4.8g

123. Green Beans

Preparation time: five mins

Cooking time: ten mins

Servings: five

Ingredients:

- half tsp. of red pepper flakes
- two tbsps. of additional-virgin olive oil
- two garlic cloves, crushed
- one and a half pounds green beans, clipped
- two tbsps. of water
- half tsp. kosher salt

Directions:

1. Warm oil in a saucepan on an average temp.

2. Don't forget to add the pepper flakes. Olive oil should be stirred in to ensure a coating.

3. Add the green beans in the calculation. Wait seven mins before serving.

4. Mix regularly. There ought to be a few browning on the bean surfaces.

5. Salt and garlic should now be added. Mixing constantly, cook the mixture for one min.

6. Put water into the container, then instantly seal it.

7. Continue to cook with the lid on for additional one min.

Per serving: Calories: 82kcal; Protein: 1g; Carbs: 6g; Fat: 6g

124. Fresh Strawberry Salsa

Preparation time: ten mins

Cooking time: zero mins

Servings: six to eight

Ingredients:

• half tsp. lime zest, aggravated

• two tsps. pure raw honey

• two kiwi fruit, skinned, sliced

• half cup fresh cilantro

• quarter cup fresh lime juice

• two lbs. fresh ripe strawberries, hulled, sliced

• half cup red onion, thinly sliced

• one to two jalapeños, deseeded, thinly sliced

Directions:

1. Honey, lime juice, and lime zest should all be combined inside a big dish and then thoroughly mixed.

2. After adding the remaining components, thoroughly combine everything. Conceal and let the flavours develop in the dish for some time before serving. Offer.

Per serving: Calories: 119kcal; Protein: 9.2g; Carbs: 11.7g; Fat: 4.3g

125. Roasted Parsnips

Preparation time: five mins

Cooking time: thirty mins

Servings: four

Ingredients:

• one tbsp. of additional-virgin olive oil

• two pounds parsnips

• one tsp. kosher salt

• one and a half tsps. Italian seasoning

• sliced parsley for garnishing

Directions:

1. Turn your microwave's temperature up to 400 °Fahrenheit.

2. The parsnips need to be peeled. Cube them into pieces that are one inch in size.

3. Currently, inside a container, combine the ingredients alongside the spice, salt, and oil.

4. Disperse this out onto the baking tray that you have. It ought to be done in a single sheet.

5. Roast for thirty mins. Each ten mins, give it a good mix.

6. Place on a platter and set aside. Dress the dish with chopped cilantro.

Per serving: Calories: 124kcal; Protein: 2g; Carbs: 20g; Fat: 4g

126. Mascarpone Couscous

Preparation time: fifteen mins

Cooking time: seven and a half hrs

Servings: four

Ingredients:

- one cup couscous
- three and a half cup chicken stock
- half cup mascarpone
- one tsp. salt
- one tsp. ground paprika

Directions:

1. Put the mascarpone and chicken broth within the pot, and heat the mixture until it reaches a boil.

2. Include salt and powdered paprika. Cook for one min while giving the mixture a gentle mix.

3. After removing the fluid from the flame, couscous should be added to it. After a thorough stirring, replace the cover.

4. Allow semolina for ten mins.

5. Prior to offering, give the cooked side item a thorough mix.

Per serving: Calories: 227kcal; Protein: 9.7g; Carbs: 35.4g; Fat: 4.9g

127. Parmesan Endives

Preparation time: 10 minutes

Cooking time: 20 minutes

Servings: 4

Ingredients:

- 4 endives, halved lengthwise
- 1 tablespoon lemon juice
- 1 tablespoon lemon zest, grated
- 2 tablespoons fat-free parmesan, grated
- two tbsps. olive oil
- A tweak of black pepper

Directions:

1. Whisk the endives with the lemon juice and the remaining components, excluding the parmesan, and place them in a pan for baking.

2. Bake the endives at 400 degrees F for twenty mins until the parmesan is melted over the endives, and offer.

Per serving: Calories: 71kcal; Protein: 0.9g; Carbs: 2.2g; Fat: 7.1g

128. Basil Olives Mix

Preparation time: five mins

Cooking time: zero mins

Servings: four

Ingredients:

- two tbsps. olive oil
- one tbsp. balsamic vinegar
- A tweak of black pepper
- four cups corn
- two cups black olives, eroded and shared
- one red onion, sliced
- half cup cherry tomatoes shared
- one tbsp. basil, sliced
- one tbsp. jalapeno, sliced
- two cups romaine lettuce, tattered

Directions:

1. Combine the corn using the olives, lettuce, and the other components inside a large bowl, toss thoroughly, split between plates and offer as a lateral dish.

Per serving: Calories: 290kcal; Protein: 6.2g; Carbs: 37.6g; Fat: 16.1g

129. Lemon Asparagus

Preparation time: 10 mins

Cooking time: 20 mins

Servings: four

Ingredients:

- one lb. asparagus, clipped
- two tablespoons basil pesto
- 1 tablespoon lemon juice
- A pinch of black pepper
- 3 tablespoons olive oil
- 2 tablespoons cilantro, chopped

Directions:

1. Arrange the asparagus n a lined baking sheet, add the pesto and the remaining components, whisk, bake at 400 °F within 20 mins.

2. Serve as a side dish.

Per serving: Calories: 114kcal; Protein: 2.6g; Carbs: 4.5g; Fat: 10.7g

130. Crispy Corn

Preparation time: eight mins

Cooking time: five mins

Servings: three

Ingredients:

- one cup corn kernels
- one tbsp. coconut flour
- half tsp. salt
- three tbsps. canola oil
- half tsp. ground paprika
- three-quarter tsp. chili pepper
- one tbsp. water

Directions:

1. Corn kernels, a pinch of salt and some coconut flour should all be mixed simultaneously in the blending basin.

2. After adding the water, thoroughly combine the maize using the spatula as a tool.

3. Canola oil will need to be heated in the pan after it has been poured in.

4. Roast it for four mins after adding the combination of corn kernels. Make sure to give it a mix every so often.

5. Once the corn kernels have reached the desired level of crunchiness, place them on a platter and pat them dry with the paper towel.

6. To taste, add ground paprika and chilli pepper. Toss everything together thoroughly.

Per serving: Calories: 179kcal; Protein: 2.1g; Carbs: 11.3g; Fat: 15g

CHAPTER 8
SNACKS

131. Toasted Pumpkin Seeds

Preparation time: five mins

Cooking time: thirty mins

Servings: two to four

Ingredients:

- one-two cups pumpkin seeds
- Water
- one tsp. salt
- half tsp. additional virgin olive oil
- Sea salt

Directions:

1. Place the seeds inside a pot and add enough water to submerge them. Include salt.

2. Raise it up to a simmer, and then keep it going for another ten mins.

3. Simmer undisturbed for additional ten mins. Once cooked, the seeds end up extremely crispy as a result of this. After draining the seeds, wipe them thoroughly with a paper towel.

4. First, line a baking tray using parchment paper, and afterwards scatter the seeds out in a uniform layer on the baking tray.

5. Sprinkle with salt, afterwards roast in a microwave preheated to 325 degrees Fahrenheit for around ten mins, mixing once midway via the cooking process.

6. Once it has cooled, place it in a secure receptacle.

Per serving: Calories: 192kcal; Protein: 10.4g; Carbs: 4.3g; Fat: 16.2g

132. Easy Guacamole

Preparation time: ten mins

Cooking time: zero mins

Servings: three

Ingredients:

- four Avocados, shared and eroded
- one tsp. Garlic Powder
- half tsp. Sea Salt

Directions:

1. Remove the interior of your avocado and place it inside a container for later use.

2. Mix in the garlic powder and salt, continuing to pulverise till the mixture is smooth. It will stay edible for up to two days if stored in the refrigerator.

Per serving: Calories: 358kcal; Protein: 7.2g; Carbs: 13.3g; Fat: 32.3g

133. Cabbage Apple Stir-Fry

Preparation time: fifteen mins

Cooking time: ten mins

Servings: 4

Ingredients:

- Two tbsps. extra-virgin olive oil
- 3 cups chopped red cabbage
- Two tablespoons water
- 1 Granny Smith apple, chopped
- Three scallions, both white and green parts, chopped
- One tablespoon freshly squeezed lemon juice
- One teaspoon caraway seed
- Pinch salt

Directions:

1. In a big skillet or frying pan, heat the olive oil over medium-high temperature.

2. Add the cabbage and stir-fry for 2 minutes. Add the water, cover, and cook for 2 minutes.

3. Uncover and stir in the apple and scallions and sprinkle with the lemon juice, caraway seeds, and salt—Stir-fry for 4 to 6 minutes longer, or until the cabbage is crisp-tender.

Per serving: Calories: 106kcal; Protein: 1g; Carbs: 11g; Fat: 7g

134. Cashew "Humus"

Preparation time: ten mins

Cooking time: zero mins

Servings: one

Ingredients:

• one Cup Cashews, Raw & Drenched in Water for fifteen mins and wearied

• two Cloves Garlic

• quarter Cup Water

• one tbsp. Olive Oil

• one tsp. Lemon juice, Fresh

• two tsp. Coconut Aminos

• half tsp. Ground Ginger

• tweak Cayenne Pepper

• quarter tsp. Sea Salt, Fine

Directions:

1. Within a blender, combine the entire components, making careful for scraping down the ends. Keep blending it till it reaches a creamy consistency, and afterwards chill it in the refrigerator prior to offering.

Per serving: Calories: 112kcal; Protein: 2.1g; Carbs: 5.4g; Fat: 8.6g

135. Apple Crisp

Preparation time: fifteen mins

Cooking time: twenty-five mins

Servings: six to eight

Ingredients:

Seasoning:

• one and a half cups old-fashioned rolled oats

• two-third cup tattered, unsweetened coconut

• one tsp. salt

• half cup stevia

• one-third cup almond meal

• quarter tsp. ground nutmeg

• two tsps. ground cinnamon

• one cup nuts, coarsely sliced

• three tbsps. dissolved coconut oil

Apple filling:

• ten tart apples

• half cup stevia

• two tbsps. fresh-embraced lemon juice

• one tbsp. ground cinnamon

• quarter cup arrowroot flour

• quarter tsp. salt

• three tbsps. dissolved coconut oil

• one tsp. vanilla

• one orange zest

Directions:

1. First, preheat the microwave to 350 degrees Fahrenheit, and afterwards oil a baking sheet measuring nine by thirteen inches alongside coconut oil.

2. Place all of the seasoning components into a dish, give it a good combine, and afterwards put it away.

3. In an instant, much larger dish, combine the components for the filling, with the exception of the apples.

4. If you want, you can keep the apple skins on the fruits. Remove the core, then cut them very thinly (about one-eighth of an inch dense).

5. To ensure a uniform coating, whisk the apples in the components for the mixture. Put the apple solution in a baking dish, then disperse the seasoning across it and press it down tightly. Bake the crisp until the seasoning is golden brown.

6. Put in the microwave while ensuring that there is a tray or pot below to collect any drippings.

7. Bake for about twenty-five mins, or till the liquids are bubbling and the seasoning is golden brown. Apples ought to have a yielding texture.

8. After allowing it to mildly cool on a tray, offer it.

Per serving: Calories: 446kcal; Protein: 6.1g; Carbs: 57.4g; Fat: 27.3g

136. Celery and Fennel Salad with Cranberries

Preparation time: fifteen mins

Cooking time: zero mins

Servings: six

Ingredients:

- quarter cup additional-virgin olive oil
- Two tbsps. newly embraced lemon juice
- One tablespoon Dijon mustard
- 2 cups sliced celery
- ½ cup chopped fennel
- ½ cup dried cranberries
- Two tablespoons minced celery leaves

Directions:

1. In a serving bowl, paddle the olive oil, lemon juice, and mustard.

2. Add the celery, fennel, and cranberries to the dressing and toss to coat. Sprinkle with the celery leaves and serve.

Per serving: Calories: 130kcal; Protein: 1g; Carbs: 13g; Fat: 9g

137. Salt & Vinegar Kale Crisps

Preparation time: five mins

Cooking time: twenty to twenty-five mins

Servings: two

Ingredients:

- four Cups Kale, ragged into two Inch Parts
- two Tbsps. Olive Oil
- two Tbsps. Apple Cider Vinegar
- one Tsp. Sea Salt, Fine

Directions:

1. Prepare your microwave by setting the temperature to 350 degrees. Bring out a dish to use for mixing, and get the entire components in there.

2. Your broccoli should be baked for twenty to twenty-five mins after being placed on a baking tray. Whisk something at the midway point of this round.

3. Place in a receptacle that can seal tightly at ambient temp. They can be stored for up to two days.

Per serving: Calories: 135kcal; Protein: 1g; Carbs: 12g; Fat: 1g

138. Spiced Nuts

Preparation time: ten mins

Cooking time: ten to fifteen mins

Servings: two

Ingredients:

• half Cup Walnuts

• one Cup Almonds

• one Tsp. Ground Turmeric

• quarter Cup Sunflower Seeds

• quarter Cup Pumpkin Puree

• quarter Tsp. Garlic Powder

• half Tsp. Ground Cumin

• quarter Tsp. Red Pepper Flakes

Directions:

1. Put the microwave on to 350 degrees to get started.

2. First, mix the entire components, and afterwards take out a sheet pan to use for roasting. Cook the almonds for ten to fifteen mins after spreading them out in a single layer on the baking tray. Wait until it has completely cooled down prior to putting it away.

Per serving: Calories: 180kcal; Protein: 3g; Carbs: 20g; Fat: 1g

139. Roasted Garlic Chickpeas

Preparation time: five mins

Cooking time: twenty mins

Servings: two

Ingredients:

• four Cups Cooked Chickpeas, washed, wearied and Dried

• one Tsp. Garlic Powder

• one Tsp. Sea Salt

• Black Pepper, as required

• two Tbsps. Olive Oil

Directions:

1. To get started, preheat your microwave to 400 degrees.

2. Place the chickpeas in an even layer onto a baking tray, then drizzle the olive oil over them.

3. Cook for a total of twenty mins, trying careful to mix the ingredients at the ten min mark of the cooking time.

4. Put your hot chickpeas inside a container, then top them and put them in a receptacle with a lid that will keep out air. They can be stored at ambient temp. for almost two days without losing their freshness.

Per serving: Calories: 150kcal; Protein: 4g; Carbs: 2g; Fat: 2g

140. Mushroom Chips

Preparation time: ten mins

Cooking time: forty-five to sixty mins

Servings: two to four

Ingredients:

• sixteen oz. of king oyster mushrooms

• two tbsps. ghee

• Kosher salt and ground pepper, as required

Directions:

1. After preheating the microwave to 300 degrees Fahrenheit, prepare two cookie dishes by lining them using parchment paper.

2. After cutting each mushroom in half longitudinally, use a mandolin to cut it into strips or pieces that are one-eighth of an inch thick. Put them in the oven on baking trays, leaving some space among each one. After the ghee has melted, season the mushrooms with the salt and pepper and afterwards spread it across the top of the mushrooms.

3. Bake them for around forty-five mins and up to one hr, or till they have reached the desired level of crispiness. Place in receptacles that are sealed.

Per serving: Calories: 62kcal; Protein: 5.5g; Carbs: 7.9g; Fat: 4g

CHAPTER 9
DESSERTS

141. Sweet Potato Muffins

Preparation time: fifteen mins

Cooking time: twenty to twenty-five mins

Servings: twelve

Ingredients:

- one Cup Sweet Potato, Cooked & Pureed
- one and a half Cups Rolled Oats
- one Tsp. Baking Powder
- half Tsp. Baking Soda
- one-third Cup Coconut Sugar
- one Cup Almond Milk
- quarter Cup Almond Butter
- one Egg
- two Tbsps. Olive Oil
- one Tsp. Ground Cinnamon
- one Tsp. Vanilla Extract, Pure
- quarter Tsp. Sea Salt

Directions:

1. Prepare your microwave by setting the temperature to 375 degrees.

2. Put paper liners in your muffin pan, and grab a mixing bowl from the cabinet.

3. Beat your oats till it makes a course flour. It should first be placed in a small container after which it should be put aside.

4. To a blender or food processor, include the entire components, with the exception of the oat flour, and puree till uniform.

5. Inside a slow, steady stream, put in your oat flour, grinding the food processor till it is completely integrated.

6. Make cuts in your cupcake containers, then place them in the oven for twenty to twenty-five mins. Prior to serving, you should wait around five mins for them to settle down.

Per serving: Calories: 143kcal; Protein: 6g; Carbs: 1g; Fat: 3g

142. Anti-Inflammatory Key Lime Pie

Preparation time: twenty mins + thirty-five mins refrigerator time

Cooking time: zero mins

Servings: eight

Ingredients:

- one cup walnuts
- one cup unsweetened ragged coconut
- quarter tsp. sea salt
- half cup Medjool dates, sliced & eroded
- three firm avocados
- half cup honey
- three tbsps. lime juice
- one tsp. lime zest
- tweak of sea salt
- Lime pieces

Directions:

1. Put the walnuts, coconut, and salt into a mixing bowl, and procedure the ingredients till they form a grainy powder.

2. Place the dates in the food processor, and continue to do so till the solution resembles bread crumbs and is attempting to come together.

3. Applying pressure will help the solution adhere to the sides and lower part of a

pie plate with a non-stick coating that has been oiled. Make the crust into a uniform layer by pressing it down with the tips of your fingertips or the back of a spatula. Whilst you are making the mixture, place the crust in the freezer for around fifiteen mins.

4. Make another pass through the mixing bowl with the avocado, honey, lime juice, lime zest, and salt, and incorporate the ingredients. To a uniform consistency, procedure.

5. After the piecrust has been refrigerated, put the filling into it and put the pie in the fridge for another twenty mins.

6. Serve the cocktail chilled, garnished with fresh lime segments. Put any leftovers in the fridge to keep them fresh.

Per serving: Calories: 273kcal; Protein: 4.1g; Carbs: 28.4g; Fat: 18.1g

143. Almonds and Oats Pudding

Preparation time: 10 minutes

Cooking time: 15 minutes

Servings: 4

Ingredients:

- 1 tbsp. lemon juice
- Zest of 1 lime
- 1 and ½ C. almond milk
- 1 tsp. almond extract
- ½ C. oats
- 2 tbsp. stevia
- ½ C. silver almonds, chopped

Directions:

1. In a pan, combine the almond milk with the lime zest and the other ingredients, whisk, bring to a simmer and cook over medium heat for 15 minutes.

2. Divide the mix into bowls and serve cold.

Per serving: Calories: 174kcal; Protein: 4g; Carbs: 3g; Fat: 12g

144. Chocolate Cups

Preparation time: 2 hours

Cooking time: 0 minutes

Servings: 6

Ingredients:

- ½ C. avocado oil
- 1 C., chocolate, melted
- 1 tsp. matcha powder
- 3 tbsp. stevia

Directions:

1. In a bowl, mix the chocolate with the oil and the rest of the ingredients, whisk really well, divide into cups and keep in the freezer for 2 hours before serving.

Per serving: Calories: 174kcal; Protein: 2g; Carbs: 3g; Fat: 9g

145. Pineapple Pudding

Preparation time: ten mins

Cooking time: 40minutes

Servings: four

Ingredients:

- 3 C. almond flour
- ¼ C. olive oil
- 1 tsp. vanilla extract
- 2 and ¼ C. stevia
- 3 eggs, whisked
- 1 and ¼ C. natural apple sauce

- 2 tsp. baking powder
- 1 and ¼ C. almond milk
- 2 C. pineapple, chopped
- Cooking spray

Directions:

1. In a bowl, combine the almond flour with the oil and the rest of the ingredients except the cooking spray and stir well.

2. Grease a cake pan with the cooking spray, pour the pudding mix inside, introduce it in the oven and bake at 370°F for 40 minutes.

3. Serve the pudding cold.

Per serving: Calories: 223kcal; Protein: 8g; Carbs: 7g; Fat: 8g

146. Ruby Pears Delight

Preparation time: 10 mins

Cooking time: ten mins

Servings: four

Ingredients:

- four pears
- 26 oz. grape juice
- 11 oz. currant jelly
- 4 garlic cloves
- Juice and zest of 1 lemon
- 4 peppercorns
- 2 rosemary springs
- ½ vanilla bean

Directions:

1. Put the jelly and grape juice in your instant pan and mix with lemon zest and juice

2. In the mix, dip each pear and wrap them in a clean tin foil and place them orderly in the steamer basket of your instant pot

3. Combine peppercorns, rosemary, garlic cloves, and vanilla bean to the juice mixture,

4. Seal the lid and cook at High for 10 minutes.

5. Release the pressure quickly, and carefully open the lid; bring out the pears, remove wrappers and arrange them on plates. Serve when cold with toppings of cooking juice.

Per serving: Calories: 145kcal; Protein: 1g; Carbs: 1g; Fat: 5g

147. Mango Bowls

Preparation time: thirty mins

Cooking time: zero mins

Servings: four

Ingredients:

- three C. mango, sliced into average chunks
- ½ C. coconut water
- ¼ C. stevia
- one tsp. vanilla extract

Directions:

1. In a blender, combine the mango with the rest of the ingredients, pulse well, divide into bowls and serve cold.

Per serving: Calories: 122kcal; Protein: 4g; Carbs: 6g; Fat: 5g

148. Mango Mug Cake

Preparation time: five mins

Cooking time: ten mins

Servings: two

Ingredients:

- one medium-sized mango, skinned & diced
- 2 eggs
- one tsp. vanilla
- ¼ tsp. nutmeg, grated
- 1 tbsp. cocoa powder
- 2 tbsp. honey
- ½ C. coconut flour

Directions:

1. Combine the coconut flour, eggs, honey, vanilla, nutmeg, and cocoa powder in 2 lightly greased mugs.

2. Then, add 1 C. of water and a metal trivet to the Instant Pot. Lower the uncovered mugs onto the trivet.

3. Put the cover on tight. Select the "Manual" option, then set the pressure to high, and set the cooking time for ten mins. After the cooking process is finished, perform a rapid pressure release and cautiously eliminate the cover.

4. Top with diced mango and serve chilled.

Per serving: Calories: 268kcal; Protein: 10g; Carbs: 34g; Fat: 10g

149. Honey Stewed Apples

Preparation time: 5 minutes

Cooking time: 5 minutes

Servings: 4

Ingredients:

- 2 tbsp. honey
- 1 tsp. cinnamon, ground
- ½ tsp. cloves, ground
- 4 apples

Directions:

1. Include the entire components to the inner pot. Now, pour in ⅓ C. of water.

2. Put the cover on tight. Select the "Manual" option, then set the pressure to high, and set the cooking time for two mins. After the cooking process is finished, perform a rapid pressure release and cautiously eliminate the cover.

3. Serve in separate containers. Bon appétit!

Per serving: Calories: 128kcal; Protein: 0g; Carbs: 34g; Fat: 0g

150. Pumpkin Pie Hummus

Preparation time: ten mins

Cooking time: ten mins

Servings: four

Ingredients:

- two C. white beans, soaked and cooked
- ½ C. homemade pumpkin purée
- 2 tbsp. almond butter
- 2 tbsp. olive oil, cold-pressed
- 1 tbsp. raw honey
- 1 tsp. cinnamon, ground
- ½ tsp. mineral salt

Directions:

1. In a food processor or high-speed blender, add all of the ingredients and blend 'til smooth. If it is too thick, add a splash of water.

2. Serve with sliced apples for dipping.

Per serving: Calories: 270kcal; Protein: 2g; Carbs: 21g; Fat: 1g

Conversion Chart

Volume Equivalents (Liquid)

US Standard	US Standard (ounces)	Metric (approximate)
2 tablespoons	1 fl. oz.	30 mL
¼ cup	2 fl. oz.	60 mL
½ cup	4 fl. oz.	120 mL
1 cup	8 fl. oz.	240 mL
1½ cups	12 fl. oz.	355 mL
2 cups or 1 pint	16 fl. oz.	475 mL
4 cups or 1 quart	32 fl. oz.	1 L
1 gallon	128 fl. oz.	4 L

Volume Equivalents (Dry)

US Standard	Metric (approximate)
⅛ teaspoon	0.5 mL
¼ teaspoon	1 mL
½ teaspoon	2 mL
¾ teaspoon	4 mL
1 teaspoon	5 mL
1 tablespoon	15 mL
¼ cup	59 mL
⅓ cup	79 mL
½ cup	118 mL
⅔ cup	156 mL
¾ cup	177 mL
1 cup	235 mL
2 cups or 1 pint	475 mL
3 cups	700 mL

4 cups or 1 quart	1 L

Oven Temperatures

Fahrenheit (F)	Celsius (C) (approximate)
250°F	120°C
300°F	150°C
325°F	165°C
350°F	180°C
375°F	190°C
400°F	200°C
425°F	220°C
450°F	230°C

Weight Equivalents

US Standard	Metric (approximate)
1 tablespoon	15 g
½ ounce	15 g
1 ounce	30 g
2 ounces	60 g
4 ounces	115 g
8 ounces	225 g
12 ounces	340 g
16 ounces or 1 pound	455 g

12 – Week Anty Meal Plan

1st Week

Days	Breakfast	Lunch	Dinner	Dessert
1	Mushroom and Bell Pepper Omelet	Garbanzo And Kidney Bean Salad	Pork with Olives	Sweet Potato Muffins
2	Anti-Inflammatory Porridge	Grilled Salmon Packets with Asparagus	Brown Rice Pilaf	Anti-Inflammatory Key Lime Pie
3	Gingerbread Oatmeal	Chicken Noodle Soup	Rosemary Chicken	Almonds and Oats Pudding
4	Savory Breakfast Pancakes	Hot Coconut Beans with Vegetables	Spanish Rice	Pumpkin Pie Hummus
5	Sweet and Savory Breakfast Hash	Orange Chicken Legs	Golden Mushroom Soup	Pineapple Pudding
6	Scrambled Eggs with Smoked Salmon	Squash Green Pea Soup	Salmon Broccoli Bowl	Chocolate Cups
7	Buckwheat Waffles	Pork with Thyme Sweet Potatoes	Basic Beans	Mango Mug Cake

2nd Week

Days	Breakfast	Lunch	Dinner	Dessert
1	Healthy Chickpea Scramble Stuffed Sweet Potatoes	Beet Haddock Dinner	Coconut Rice with Berries	Sweet Potato Muffins
2	Chia Breakfast Pudding	Chicken Squash Soup	Pork Chops with Tomato Salsa	Pumpkin Pie Hummus
3	Cucumber Bites	Mushroom Tacos	Coconut Cashew Soup with Butternut Squash	Mango Mug Cake
4	Smoked Salmon Scrambled Eggs	Lemon and Cilantro Rice	Mustard Pork Mix	Chocolate Cups

5	Blueberry Breakfast Blend	Chipotle Squash Soup	Wasabi Salmon Burgers	Almonds and Oats Pudding
6	Breakfast Burgers with Avocado Buns	Parsley Pork and Artichokes	Habanero Pinto Bean and Bell Pepper Pot	Honey Stewed Apples
7	Appetizing Crepes with Berries	Scrumptious Coconut Shrimps	Stuffed Pepper Soup	Ruby Pears Delight

3rd Week

Days	Breakfast	Lunch	Dinner	Dessert
1	Coconut Pancakes	Brown Rice and Chicken Soup	Ginger and Chili Sea Bass Fillets	Mango Mug Cake
2	Spinach Fritters	Quick Quinoa with Cinnamon and Chia	Pork and Leeks	Ruby Pears Delight
3	Granola	Zucchini Noodles with Spring Vegetables	Roasted Red Pepper and Eggplant Soup	Pineapple Pudding
4	Oats with Berries	Cranberry Pork	Mushroom Risotto with Spring Peas	Mango Bowls
5	Fruity Bowl	Zesty Broccoli Soup	Honey Scallops	Anti-Inflammatory Key Lime Pie
6	Oatmeal Pancakes	Fresh Tuna Steak and Fennel Salad	White Bean, Chicken & Apple Cider Chili	Honey Stewed Apples
7	Fruity Bowl	Pork with Pears and Ginger	Italian Wedding Soup	Sweet Potato Muffins

4th Week

Days	Breakfast	Lunch	Dinner	Dessert
1	Spinach Fritters	Roasted Carrot Soup	Beef with Carrot & Broccoli	Anti-Inflammatory Key Lime Pie

2	Savory Breakfast Pancakes	Braised Kale	Quinoa Salmon Bowl	Mango Mug Cake
3	Mushroom and Bell Pepper Omelet	Pork Kabobs with Bell Peppers	Beef & Vegetable Soup	Almonds and Oats Pudding
4	Buckwheat Waffles	Spicy Quinoa	Pork with Chili Zucchinis and Tomatoes	Mango Bowls
5	Cucumber Bites	Chicken And Tortilla Soup	Vinegar Spiced Salmon with Honey	Chocolate Cups
6	Oats with Berries	Citrus Salmon on A Bed of Greens	Taco Soup	Honey Stewed Apples
7	Sweet and Savory Breakfast Hash	Bean and Rice Casserole	Lamb with Prunes	Sweet Potato Muffins

5th Week

Days	Breakfast	Lunch	Dinner	Dessert
1	Chia Breakfast Pudding	Fennel Baked Cod	Healthy Vegetable Fried Rice	Pineapple Pudding
2	Gingerbread Oatmeal	Chicken Noodle Soup	Roasted Chicken	Almonds and Oats Pudding
3	Coconut Pancakes	Celery and Turmeric Lentils	Herbed Mussels Treat	Mango Mug Cake
4	Scrambled Eggs with Smoked Salmon	Lime Spinach and Chickpeas Salad	Golden Mushroom Soup	Pumpkin Pie Hummus
5	Healthy Chickpea Scramble Stuffed Sweet Potatoes	Smokey Turkey Chili	Rice & Currant Salad Mediterranean Style	Chocolate Cups
6	Anti-Inflammatory Porridge	Chipotle Squash Soup	Spicy Veggie Pancakes	Anti-Inflammatory Key Lime Pie
7	Granola	Coconut Chili Salmon	Grandma's Black Bean Chili	Ruby Pears Delight

6th Week

Days	Breakfast	Lunch	Dinner	Dessert
1	Appetizing Crepes with Berries	Chicken Squash Soup	Spiced Ground Beef	Pineapple Pudding
2	Breakfast Burgers with Avocado Buns	Herbed Harvest Rice	Honey Scallops	Anti-Inflammatory Key Lime Pie
3	Oatmeal Pancakes	Brown Rice Pilaf	Zesty Broccoli Soup	Honey Stewed Apples
4	Smoked Salmon Scrambled Eggs	Onion and Orange Healthy Salad	Southern Bean Bowl	Almonds and Oats Pudding
5	Blueberry Breakfast Blend	Garbanzo And Kidney Bean Salad	Southern Bean Bowl	Mango Bowls
6	Coconut Pancakes	Coconut Cashew Soup with Butternut Squash	Garlic Cod Meal	Sweet Potato Muffins
7	Oats with Berries	Roasted Portobellos with Rosemary	Taco Soup	Pumpkin Pie Hummus

7th Week

Days	Breakfast	Lunch	Dinner	Dessert
1	Gingerbread Oatmeal	Orange and Maple-Glazed Salmon	Basic Beans	Chocolate Cups
2	Buckwheat Waffles	Roasted Red Pepper and Eggplant Soup	Turkey Sausages	Sweet Potato Muffins
3	Anti-Inflammatory Porridge	Herbed Harvest Rice	Cauliflower Mashed Potatoes	Ruby Pears Delight
4	Sweet and Savory Breakfast Hash	Cilantro and Avocado Platter	Brown Rice and Chicken Soup	Almonds and Oats Pudding
5	Scrambled Eggs with Smoked Salmon	Mushroom Risotto With Spring Peas	Ground Chicken and Peas Curry	Mango Mug Cake
6	Blueberry Breakfast Blend	Italian Wedding Soup	Kale Cod Secret	Anti-Inflammatory Key Lime Pie

7	Savory Breakfast Pancakes	Oregano Pork	Roasted Carrot Soup	Honey Stewed Apples

8th Week

Days	Breakfast	Lunch	Dinner	Dessert
1	Appetizing Crepes with Berries	Stuffed Pepper Soup	Lime-Salmon Patties	Almonds and Oats Pudding
2	Mushroom and Bell Pepper Omelet	Pork Chops with Tomato Salsa	Hot Coconut Beans with Vegetables	Mango Bowls
3	Smoked Salmon Scrambled Eggs	Vegetable Potpie	Chicken and Tortilla Soup	Mango Mug Cake
4	Cucumber Bites	Rice & Currant Salad Mediterranean Style	Cranberry Pork	Pineapple Pudding
5	Healthy Chickpea Scramble Stuffed Sweet Potatoes	Squash Green Pea Soup	Paprika Brussels Sprouts	Pumpkin Pie Hummus
6	Spinach Fritters	Halibut Curry	White Bean, Chicken & Apple Cider Chili	Honey Stewed Apples
7	Chia Breakfast Pudding	Orange Chicken Legs	Beef & Vegetable Soup	Sweet Potato Muffins

9th Week

Days	Breakfast	Lunch	Dinner	Dessert
1	Granola	Zesty Broccoli Soup	Pork with Pears and Ginger	Anti-Inflammatory Key Lime Pie
2	Breakfast Burgers with Avocado Buns	Sweet Potato Puree	Celery and Turmeric Lentils	Sweet Potato Muffins
3	Oatmeal Pancakes	Pork with Thyme Sweet Potatoes	Italian Wedding Soup	Ruby Pears Delight

4	Fruity Bowl	Brown Rice and Chicken Soup	Miso-Glazed Salmon	Almonds and Oats Pudding
5	Spinach Fritters	Grandma's Black Bean Chili	Pork Kabobs with Bell Peppers	Chocolate Cups
6	Chia Breakfast Pudding	Mustard Pork Mix	Roasted Red Pepper and Eggplant Soup	Mango Mug Cake
7	Sweet and Savory Breakfast Hash	Taco Soup	Salmon Ceviche	Honey Stewed Apples

10th Week

Days	Breakfast	Lunch	Dinner	Dessert
1	Savory Breakfast Pancakes	Beef & Vegetable Soup	Curried Okra	Mango Bowls
2	Blueberry Breakfast Blend	Coconut Rice with Berries	Spanish Rice	Sweet Potato Muffins
3	Mushroom and Bell Pepper Omelet	Beet Haddock Dinner	Chicken Squash Soup	Anti-Inflammatory Key Lime Pie
4	Buckwheat Waffles	Beef with Carrot & Broccoli	Quick Quinoa with Cinnamon and Chia	Pineapple Pudding
5	Oats with Berries	Coconut Cashew Soup with Butternut Squash	Stir-Fried Almond and Spinach	Mango Mug Cake
6	Gingerbread Oatmeal	Healthy Vegetable Fried Rice	Pork with Chili Zucchinis and Tomatoes	Chocolate Cups
7	Cucumber Bites	Coconut Chili Salmon	Roasted Carrot Soup	Pumpkin Pie Hummus

11th Week

Days	Breakfast	Lunch	Dinner	Dessert
1	Scrambled Eggs with Smoked Salmon	Squash Green Pea Soup	Roasted Chicken	Almonds and Oats Pudding

2	Healthy Chickpea Scramble Stuffed Sweet Potatoes	Spicy Wasabi Mayonnaise	Chipotle Squash Soup	Pineapple Pudding
3	Breakfast Burgers with Avocado Buns	Habanero Pinto Bean and Bell Pepper Pot	Salmon Broccoli Bowl	Mango Bowls
4	Anti-Inflammatory Porridge	Stuffed Pepper Soup	Spiced Ground Beef	Honey Stewed Apples
5	Smoked Salmon Scrambled Eggs	Pork with Olives	Broccoli with Garlic and Lemon	Pumpkin Pie Hummus
6	Granola	Scrumptious Coconut Shrimps	Chicken Noodle Soup	Ruby Pears Delight
7	Coconut Pancakes	Lemon and Cilantro Rice	Wasabi Salmon Burgers	Pumpkin Pie Hummus

12th Week

Days	Breakfast	Lunch	Dinner	Dessert
1	Appetizing Crepes with Berries	Grilled Salmon Packets with Asparagus	Taco Soup	Almonds and Oats Pudding
2	Oatmeal Pancakes	Golden Mushroom Soup	Black-Eyed Peas and Greens Power Salad	Ruby Pears Delight
3	Fruity Bowl	Smokey Turkey Chili	Bean and Rice Casserole	Anti-Inflammatory Key Lime Pie
4	Chia Breakfast Pudding	Salmon Ceviche	Chicken and Tortilla Soup	Mango Bowls
5	Oats with Berries	Quinoa Salmon Bowl	Ground Chicken and Peas Curry	Pineapple Pudding
6	Savory Breakfast Pancakes	Chicken Noodle Soup	Turmeric Endives	Chocolate Cups

7	Blueberry Breakfast Blend	Oregano Pork	Spicy Quinoa	Sweet Potato Muffins

Conclusion

The anti-inflammatory diet is one of the best and healthiest diets. If you want to stay healthy, follow an anti-inflammatory diet. You should eat fresh fruits, fresh vegetables, gluten-free foods, lean meat, fish, gluten-free grains, nuts, seeds, and many more in this diet. You can check parts of What to Eat and What To Avoid in this cookbook. If you have any inflammatory symptoms, you should go to your doctor, who will accordingly give your food tips. And thus you can adjust your own diet with the assistance of this cookbook. Good diet habits should also be token, like drinking plenty of water, choose healthy snacks, consume healthy fats and proteins, and avoid fast, processed, and junk foods.

In this cookbook, you will find easy, healthy, and delicious recipes. In this book, anything you can imagine in a cookbook includes breakfast recipes, vegetables, meat, fish, soups, desserts, snacks recipes, and many more. It is a good option for your health. All recipes are simple to cook and easy to follow. You don't even need any special ingredients or equipment to make them. Thank you for choosing this cookbook and making us feel honored. Stay healthy, stay hydrated, and stay anti-inflammatory!

Index

Mustard Pork Mix; 48
Oatmeal Pancakes; 25
Oats with Berries; 19
Onion and Orange Healthy Salad; 67
Orange and Maple-Glazed Salmon; 62
Orange Chicken Legs; 46
Oregano Pork; 51
Paprika Brussels Sprouts; 73
Parmesan Endives; 81
Parsley Pork and Artichokes; 45
Pineapple Pudding; 91
Pork and Leeks; 54
Pork Chops with Tomato Salsa; 48
Pork Kabobs with Bell Peppers; 53
Pork with Chili Zucchinis and Tomatoes; 51
Pork with Olives; 47
Pork with Pears and Ginger; 52
Pork with Thyme Sweet Potatoes; 47
Pumpkin Pie Hummus; 93
Quick Quinoa with Cinnamon and Chia; 42
Quinoa Salmon Bowl; 41
Rice & Currant Salad Mediterranean Style; 37
Roasted Carrot Soup; 32
Roasted Carrots; 77
Roasted Chicken; 46
Roasted Garlic Chickpeas; 87
Roasted Parsnips; 80
Roasted Portobellos With Rosemary; 68
Roasted Red Pepper and Eggplant Soup; 29
Rosemary Chicken; 47
Ruby Pears Delight; 92
Salmon Broccoli Bowl; 65
Salmon Ceviche; 59

Salt & Vinegar Kale Crisps; 86
Savory Breakfast Pancakes; 18
Scrambled Eggs with Smoked Salmon; 19
Scrumptious Coconut Shrimps; 64
Smoked Salmon Scrambled Eggs; 23
Smokey Turkey Chili; 49
Southern Bean Bowl; 39
Spanish Rice; 38
Spiced Ground Beef; 45
Spiced Nuts; 87
Spicy Quinoa; 42
Spicy Veggie Pancakes; 70
Spicy Wasabi Mayonnaise; 69
Spinach Fritters; 25
Squash Green Pea Soup; 28
Stir-Fried Almond And Spinach; 75
Stir-Fried Squash; 71
Stuffed Pepper Soup; 30
Sweet and Savory Breakfast Hash; 22
Sweet Potato Muffins; 90
Sweet Potato Puree; 69
Taco Soup; 28
Toasted Pumpkin Seeds; 84
Tomato Bulgur; 77
Turkey Sausages; 52
Turmeric Endives; 67
Vegetable Potpie; 73
Vinegar Spiced Salmon with Honey; 60
Wasabi Salmon Burgers; 56
White Bean, Chicken & Apple Cider Chili; 40
Zesty Broccoli Soup; 28
Zucchini Noodles with Spring Vegetables; 72